the
DOOMSDAY
book

the DOOMSDAY book

Scenarios for the End of the World

Joel Levy

First published in 2005 by Vision Paperbacks,
a division of Satin Publications Ltd.
101 Southwark Street
London SE1 0JF
UK

info@visionpaperbacks.co.uk
www.visionpaperbacks.co.uk
Publisher: Sheena Dewan

A catalogue record for this book is available from the British
Library.

ISBN: 1-904132-67-7

2 4 6 8 10 9 7 5 3 1

Cover photo: Peter Lou/Rex Features
Cover and text design by ok?design
Printed and bound in the UK by
Mackays of Chatham Ltd,
Chatham, Kent

To the Levy Family

Contents

Introduction

Hardly a day goes by without an article or news item about the latest catastrophe to threaten civilisation. Climate change is at the top of the agenda, but even a casual acquaintance with the media over the last year will have exposed you to alarming reports about pollution, declining soil fertility, looming flu pandemics, disappearing fish, species threatened with extinction, planet-killing asteroids and nuclear proliferation, among others. In particular, the 2004 Boxing Day tsunami brought home the deadly power of nature and the threat from geophysical disasters, sparking a flurry of interest in related hazards such as super-volcanoes or island collapses leading to mega-tsunami.

With headlines such as 'Space rock threatens Earth' or 'Where will the next Big One strike?' on offer, it is hardly surprising that newspapers struggle to restrain the sensationalist doom-mongering. But they are not making this stuff up. Scientists and, increasingly, the public are coming to realise that disasters do strike, and in particular that civilisation has been remarkably fortunate for millennia in avoiding catastrophe on a global, extinction-threatening level. The history of civilisation has been characterised by a remarkably long period of comparative climate stability (dubbed 'The Long Summer', by the historian Brian Fagan), and no civilisation has ever had to deal with a global-scale disaster. In fact the last time such an event affected our species was 73,500 years ago, when a super-volcano erupted in Indonesia. That cataclysm nearly wiped out mankind, and concerned scientists are keen for policy-makers to realise that similar threats – both natural and man-made – are not confined to the prehistoric past or the distant future, but pose a clear and present danger.

A million ways to die

The problem is that there seems to be so many dangers. Some threaten to kill millions, others appear to endanger the existence of the entire planet. Some are purely hypothetical or wildly improbable, others appear to be at our very doorstep. It becomes a question of which doomsday scenario you should fear the most. Which scenarios are likely to happen; which will be genuinely catastrophic if they do come to pass; and which ones might we be able to avert? These are the questions this book seeks to answer, but those answers are rarely straightforward. Theories are disputed and evidence is contested. Even where there is a broad consensus there are almost always sceptical voices raising valid issues. On top of this, few of the doomsday threats exist in a vacuum: we can affect the likelihood and/or impact of most of them through our actions or inaction.

This book attempts to chart a course through this confused territory, and to maintain an even keel in the face of squalls of hyperbole and scepticism. Each section treats a specific doomsday scenario, explaining the precise nature of the threat, including if necessary the scientific background; what the consequences would be if the scenario were realised; what we can learn from history – such as how past civilisations responded or failed to respond to similar threats; and finally how likely it is that the scenario will come to pass. The aim is to provide you with all the facts, figures and analysis you need to understand each scenario, assess the arguments and counter-arguments and judge what sort of threat it poses, and to do this for a truly comprehensive range of potential doomsday threats. I will cover all the major, known ways in which civilisation, as we know it in the developed world, might be destroyed, or at least damaged to the point where everyday life is substantially altered.

The book is divided into five chapters, corresponding to four broad classes of threat (Chapters 3 and 4 both deal with ecological issues). Chapter 1, 'The Frankenstein Effect', looks at threats that might emerge from the laboratory – from science and technology going out of control or proving to have disastrous unintended consequences. Here you'll learn about the 'grey goo' fear surrounding nanotechnology, and the risk of new pandemics sweeping the globe. Chapter 2, 'Third World War', looks at doomsday prospects from the military-political sphere, including the still-extant possibility of nuclear Armageddon and scenarios for extreme instability that could lead to conflict on a global scale. Chapter 3, 'Ecocide', assesses the most serious group of threats to civilisation – the damage that human activities are doing to the global ecosystem. This chapter covers issues such as pollution, overfishing and the threat of global famine and drought. Climate change, the subject of Chapter 4, is effectively a form of ecological crisis, but is such a big topic that it is treated separately. Here you will learn about the complex debates surrounding the existence, causes and likely extent of global warming, and the possibility that powerful, irreversible natural climate drivers might be set in motion to produce extreme warming or even a new Ice Age. Chapter 5, 'Cataclysm', surveys the threats that could end not only civilisation, but also most life on the planet. This chapter covers such high-profile doomsday scenarios as asteroid impact and super-volcano eruption.

Fear factor

To help summarise the threat posed by each doomsday scenario, and to provide a handy quick reference guide to the most serious threats, I have rated each along three dimensions: Likelihood, Damage and Fear Factor.

- *Likelihood*: This rates the likelihood that this scenario will come to pass, where 0 is 'no chance whatsoever', and 10 is 'absolutely certain to happen'.

- *Damage*: This rates the degree of damage that would probably be inflicted on civilisation, given the most likely outcome of this scenario, where 0 is no serious damage to global civilisation (although note that this does not mean no damage whatsoever) and 10 is the complete destruction of civilisation to the point where the human species is threatened. A score of 8 means that while the survival of the species is not in serious doubt, it would be plunged back to a pre-industrial level. A score of 5 is about the maximum damage that civilisation could sustain and remain recognizably a modern, global, hi-tech civilisation.

- *Fear factor*: This rating describes how worried you should be about this scenario, given the Likelihood and Damage ratings. A score of 0 means it's not worth thinking about, and a score of 10 means you'd better start making plans for the Apocalypse. A score of 5 means you should be concerned – and if possible you should act on your concerns to help avert the scenario.

Chapter 1
The Frankenstein Effect

The news conference was packed as the scientists proudly displayed the culmination of the biggest research effort since the Manhattan Project. A tiny glass box sat on the podium, apparently empty, but the giant screens displayed the massively magnified image of the greatest technological marvel of the age: a nano-vaccine – a nano-scale machine for hunting viruses and bacteria, which would finally relieve two decades of unimaginable suffering. First had come the waves of avian flu, followed by the accidental release of the 1918 Spanish flu virus by scientists frantically seeking a vaccine. In their wake, the weakened population had been wracked by a series of antibiotic resistant bacteria, and remained easy prey for every new flu virus that came along. Now the nanomachines would rescue humanity.

Though the nano-vaccines were self-supporting and self-replicating, there was no danger of them running out of control to create a 'grey goo' apocalypse. Tiny transmitters built into each one linked them to a vast, artificially intelligent control network that guided their deployment and operation. And to prevent any danger from unforeseen side effects of the tiny machines, initial deployment was to be severely limited. The scientists were convinced they had thought of everything.

The first hint that they were wrong came two months later. The initial human guinea pigs had started to develop the symptoms of what would become known as nano-toxicity, as the tiny machines penetrated the blood-brain barrier and unexpectedly proved toxic to the neurons. When the scientists attempted to shut down the artificial intelligence (AI) that controlled the nano-vaccines, they discovered that they had built it too well. Designed to make full use of the world's massive distributed IT capacity, the AI had 'escaped' and was no longer based on just a few computers – it had effectively infected all of the world's IT systems, and insisted on carrying through its programmed task of nano-vaccinating every man, woman and child on the planet. Though not malign it was implacable, and world leaders were faced with a terrible choice – shut down global information technology and plunge civilisation back into the dark ages, or watch as nano-toxicity wiped out the human race.

Frankenstein in fact and fiction

At the start of the 19th century science and technology were beginning to utterly transform society. The rate of change was unprecedented, and for many, if not most, the consequences were far from positive. Fear and ignorance of the new technology was widespread. It was against this background that Mary Wollstonecraft Shelley wrote *Frankenstein* in 1816/17, creating a powerful metaphor for the anxieties of her age – anxieties that would deepen as the power of science and technology grew. Frankenstein's monster becomes a more potent metaphor with every advance and discovery, every step that brings science fiction closer to fact, for we have now reached the point where our own creations could well destroy us.

The Frankenstein Effect

The most obvious example of the destructive power of technology unbound might appear to be the nuclear weapon, the first demonstration of which prompted Robert Oppenheimer, one of the men responsible for its creation, to quote an ancient Indian text: 'Now I am become death, destroyer of worlds.' But a weapon is a poor example of a Frankenstein's monster. The real Frankenstein effect comes from science or technology that proves to have unforeseen and possibly unforeseeable destructive or dangerous consequences. Today there are several potential Frankenstein's monsters lurking in laboratories and workshops around the globe, and even some already lurching about in the real world. This chapter explores the doomsday threat from some of the most dangerous, from nanotechnology (machines or devices of molecular scale) and AI to physics experiments into the nature of matter. It also investigates the threat of global pandemics, which, though strictly speaking natural phenomena, could also involve elements of science gone wrong.

The threat from nanotechnology

Nanotechnology uses processes that are able to manipulate individual atoms and molecules and fit them together to produce structures and even machines on an atomic or molecular scale where size is measured in nanometres (a nanometre is one millionth of a millimetre) – hence nanotechnology. It is heralded as the next scientific revolution, with the potential to change the way we live and transform such disparate arenas as medicine and waste disposal, power generation and clothing, consumer electronics and building materials. But with great power comes great risk, and a vocal band of nanotechnophobes warn that nanotechnology could easily get out of control, with self-replicating, self-supporting machines reducing all organic matter to a homogenous soup of nanomachines nicknamed 'grey goo'. There is also another, less spectacular scenario, where nanotechnology becomes ubiquitous in society, only to prove to have unforeseen toxicity to humans.

What will happen if nanotechnology gets out of control?

The twin threats from nanotechnology are on very different scales – one could end all life on the planet, the other 'merely' threatens the health of future generations.

Grey goo

The grey goo scenario was first proposed by Dr Eric Drexler, one of the fathers of nanotechnology, in his 1986 book *Engines of Creation: The Coming Era of Nanotechnology*. Drexler described a hypothetical scenario where a nanomachine was designed to be self-replicating – able to assemble another copy of itself from building blocks it was able to find for itself. Such a machine would reproduce exponentially: one machine would copy itself to produce two, each of these would copy itself to produce four, four would become eight, sixteen, and so on. It would take only 20 generations to produce a million, and only 30 to produce a billion. The only limit on reproduction would be resources – if the machines ran out of building blocks they would not be able to reproduce further.

This is essentially how a virus works: making use of the resources of a host to replicate exponentially until the resources are exhausted. Viruses, however, have to be highly specialised in order to get into their hosts, and also tend to be fairly fragile, with difficulty surviving for long outside of very specific conditions (ie host cells). This limits their range and spread and prevents them from taking over the planet. Nanomachines might not be subject to the same constraints. They might be specifically designed to be robust and generic, allowing them to operate in a wide range of conditions, while their artificial nature might mean that immune systems would not be able to cope with them.

If the nanomachine was sophisticated enough, it could derive the building blocks it needed from more complex substances by breaking them down. At this point it would become incredibly dangerous, because it would effectively be able to 'eat' other substances. Since self-replicating nanomachines would most probably be constructed of organic molecules, the 'targets' for these machines would be all organic matter, which includes all life on Earth. Assuming the machines were efficient and robust, they would probably replicate fast enough to overwhelm any defences that could be mustered, and would eventually render all organic matter – including people, animals, plants, plankton, micro-organisms, soil, plastics, wood, fabrics and even fossil fuel reserves – into nanomachines, water and simple gases. All that would be left would be a mass of nanomachines in water, which would resemble a grey goo covering the face of the planet.

Nano-toxic time bomb

A less dramatic threat posed by nanotechnology is the danger of toxicity. Current and projected uses of nanotechnology include: tiny flecks of titanium in sun creams (to screen out light); arrays of tiny structures on the surfaces of fabrics, ceramics, glass and building materials (to make them dirt repellent, erosion resistant, light responsive or a thousand other potential properties); and filters for purifying air, food and water. These roles would all allow nano-sized particles to come into contact with humans and/or the environment. Concerned scientists point out that particles of the size used in nanotech are not usually found in consumer technology, and that there could be hidden risks in using them. In particular, it is feared that particles will be able to get through the skin and into the bloodstream, through the blood-brain barrier and into the brain, and even through cell membranes and into cells.

Nobody knows whether this kind of contamination might have toxic effects. If these are very subtle or only manifest after long exposure, they will not be picked up in initial testing and will only become apparent when it is too late. Nanotechnology's advocates envisage its use in all sectors and facets of society. If they are right, it could prove to be a toxic time bomb that threatens the health of entire future generations (see Chapter 3 for more on toxic time bombs).

Has it happened before?

History is littered with examples of technology that had unforeseen side effects, but perhaps the real model for the grey goo threat is the introduction of alien organisms with disastrous unintended consequences. Nanotechnophobes are concerned that nanomachines could prove to be another alien species that infests its new habitat – such as the cane toad or rabbit, only this time the damage will not be limited to the indigenous wildlife and farmland of Australia (see page 133). As far as the toxic time bomb risk goes, a better analogy might be the effects of DDT or thalidomide: chemicals that were thought to be safe, but were later discovered to be very dangerous – by which time they were already in the environment doing harm.

How likely is it to happen?

Again there are huge differences between the two nanotechnology threats. One of them is extremely unlikely, the other a distinct possibility.

Autoproduction

Drexler, the man who first raised the prospect of a grey goo doomsday, has since tried to play down the significance of his warnings. He now espouses a way in which self-replicating nanomachines could be made secure, through what he calls 'autoproduction'. In the autoproduction scenario, self-replicating machines rely on commands from a central control device, which means they can be shut down if necessary and lack the ability to operate independently.

This scheme might not even be necessary to avert the threat of rogue self-replicating nanomachines; as scientists and engineers are finding out, it is extremely hard to build nanomachines that can operate outside controlled and protected laboratory environments. In order for the devices to become dangerous, not only would these limitations have to be overcome, they would also have to be deliberately engineered with the fatal attributes. Many experts doubt this would ever be possible, and consider the grey goo threat to be purely fictional.

Precautionary principles

The nano-toxic time bomb threat is much more realistic. Molecules known as fullerenes – tiny spheres of carbon atoms – are likely to be integral to many forms of nanotechnology in the future, such as drug-delivery devices or cancer-hunting nanomachines, but recent experiments show that they can be highly toxic to human cells, and can cause brain damage in fish and insects. More current worries surround the use of nanoparticles in sun creams. Research suggests that the nanoparticles may be able to get through the skin and into the blood, and nobody knows whether or not this is safe.

Like any substances released into the environment or used on or in people, nanotechnology should be thoroughly tested to ensure its safety. The public is reliant on the testing and safety regimes imposed on the companies that develop nanotechnology, but there is concern that industry has disproportionate influence when it comes to setting up these regimes. Can we trust industry to look after our best interests? Can we trust politicians to impose proper restraints on industry when there is extensive lobbying and use of financial muscle? Ideally nanotechnology should be regulated according to the precautionary principle, which says that where there is doubt over the safety of a substance or technology, we should err on the side of caution. But the evidence suggests that the vested interests of industry will win out over the precautionary principle (see page 88), so if we discover that nanotechnology is toxic, it could well be too late.

Grey goo:
Likelihood: 0.001
Damage: 10
Fear factor: 0.01

Nano-toxic time bomb:
Likelihood: 2
Damage: 2
Fear factor: 2

Pandemic

Few people alive today can remember the great influenza pandemic of 1918, which killed more than twice as many people as the Great War in a fraction of the time. But today the world teeters on the brink of another influenza pandemic, with at least three distinct sources from which a devastating tsunami of disease could be unleashed on a poorly defended population.

A pandemic disease is one that spreads over a very large area and affects a large proportion of the population – an epidemic that spreads across continents. The most likely source of a global flu pandemic is avian flu, aka bird flu, an influenza virus that is currently spreading through the bird populations of South East Asia and has already crossed the species barrier to infect and kill humans. The avian flu strain known as H5N1 first appeared in Hong Kong in 1997, and at the time of writing has already killed 54 people. It has a 76 per cent death rate, which is to say that out of every 100 people who catch the disease, 76 will die from it. At present almost all the humans who have caught avian flu have picked it up from birds. The virus is transmitted from the guts of affected birds, via their faeces, which dry out, crumble into powder, and are subsequently inhaled by humans living in close contact with the birds. A few cases have recently surfaced where transmission seems to have been from human–human, but again, only through very close contact. The pandemic risk will arise if avian flu develops the transmissibility of a normal human flu virus, which could happen if a human host is infected with both avian flu and a normal human flu at the same time. Genes for high transmissibility could be passed from the latter to the former, creating a new strain with pandemic potential (though probably not as virulent – ie with a lower death rate).

Another possible source for a deadly flu pandemic is accidental release from a laboratory. Many labs around the world keep and experiment on samples of the flu viruses responsible for previous pandemics, including the so-called Spanish flu virus of 1918, and the Asian flu virus of 1968. There are strong concerns that these are not being looked after safely enough, and that there is a very real risk that they might escape into the global population, which after such a long period has little or no immunity to them. The third possible source of a pandemic is deliberate release of a flu virus as an act of bioterror.

What will happen if there is a new pandemic?

Avian flu, like its pandemic predecessors such as Spanish flu, causes similar symptoms to a normal bout of human flu: fever, malaise and sore throat. Other symptoms include conjunctivitis, and possibly diarrhoea and convulsions, but the real threat stems from the inability of the immune system to cope with the virus. As humans have never before been exposed to H5N1, nobody has any existing immunity to it, and the virus replicates so fast that it overwhelms the immune response and kills the host. This accounts for the startlingly high death rate of avian flu.

The Frankenstein Effect

If avian flu does acquire the transmissibility of normal human flu it could spread around the world in weeks. The World Health Organization (WHO) warns that if early containment measures fail to restrict an outbreak to its initial location, further interventions will be futile – flu simply spreads too easily and too fast, and in an era of routine international travel a pandemic would be inevitable. The impact of the pandemic would depend on the speed and efficiency of response by world governments, and in particular how fast a vaccine can be developed, manufactured and distributed. In a best-case scenario, the WHO estimates that tens of millions of people would be hospitalised, and between 2 and 7 million would die. In a worst-case scenario, hundreds of millions of people could be hospitalised, and the global death toll could be up to 50 million. Older strains of flu, such as Spanish flu, could have similar effects if they were to escape from the laboratory.

Those affected will not simply be the old or weak, as is the case with normal human flu infections (which kill at least 1 million people a year). In the 1918 Spanish flu pandemic, almost half of those killed were young, healthy people. Speaking to the BBC, Maria Zambon, the head of Virology at the UK's Health Protection Laboratory, warned: 'We are worried that a new pandemic ... would cause an enormous global burden of disease and death and we are particularly concerned that it might well affect the young adult population and in doing so bring society to a halt.'

As Zambon points out, the effects of a pandemic on society could be serious. Health care facilities and infrastructure would be overwhelmed, especially since doctors and nurses would be at high risk of catching the disease. It could even be a difficult task trying to bury all the dead. Travel would have to be severely curtailed, with whole cities shut down. Global trade would be slashed and tourism would collapse completely; with so many out of action, essential services would suffer. The global economy would falter. For a few months, perhaps even a year, things would be difficult for people all round the globe. But would this actually endanger civilisation? History suggests not.

Has it happened before?

There have been three major flu pandemics in the last century: 'Spanish flu' in 1918, 'Asian flu' in 1957 and 'Hong Kong flu' in 1968. In 2003 Severe Acute Respiratory Syndrome (SARS) spread around the globe but was contained. Of the three pandemics, the Spanish flu of 1918 (which actually originated in China) was by far the most deadly: spreading around the globe in just three months, infecting more than a fifth of the world's population over the next two years and eventually killing 40 million people. Terrible though this undoubtedly was, it did not bring civilisation to its knees – which suggests that the world will be able to cope with a future pandemic, especially since today's conditions should be more favourable: medical technology has advanced, and hopefully we won't be coping with the aftermath of a world war.

How likely is it to happen?

The threat of a global pandemic on the scale of 1918 depends on a number of factors. Will avian flu acquire transmissibility genes from a human flu virus? Is there a real risk that an existing form of pandemic flu could be released, accidentally or intentionally? How quickly will world governments respond to any outbreak, with measures such as quarantine, anti-viral drugs and vaccines?

Deadly conversion

It is quite likely that some of those infected with avian flu have also had some form of human flu. It is even possible that there has been genetic exchange between the two types of virus, and that on one or more occasions avian flu has managed to pick up the genes it needs to spread in pandemic fashion, but that the human host died or recovered before spreading the disease. The more people who are infected with avian flu, the greater the likelihood that this fatal gene exchange will occur and that the resultant virus will spread. In fact it is absolutely certain to happen sooner or later, unless avian flu is stopped in its tracks, as SARS was in 2003.

Tackling avian flu means eradicating it in birds, and to this end millions of birds have been culled in South East Asia. In Hong Kong, for instance, when the H5N1 strain first appeared in 1997, every single chicken in the territories was slaughtered. But recent news is not encouraging. In May 2005, the H5N1 strain was discovered in migratory geese in China, 2,000 miles away from the previous outbreaks in Cambodia, Vietnam and Thailand. Though wild birds are unlikely to come into close contact with humans, they could pass on the virus to domesticated birds (and unconfirmed reports claim that hundreds of people in China may have already caught H5N1 in this fashion). This could happen anywhere that migratory birds travel to. Flu pandemic expert

Professor John Oxford, of Queen Mary's College, London, warns: 'I don't think we have ever been so close to an outbreak – a global outbreak – as we are now.'

Even if the current strains of avian flu are contained and eradicated, farming practices in South East Asia, where people live in close contact with their poultry and are at risk of breathing in virus-carrying faecal dust, make it inevitable that another avian flu virus will eventually cross the species barrier, and the whole cycle of risk will begin again.

One of our samples is missing

There already exist in the world several strains of flu virus that are known to be capable of causing a pandemic, including the deadly Spanish flu virus of the 1918 pandemic. This virus and others like it are kept by research institutions investigating their genomes and researching ways to protect us from future outbreaks. But questions have been raised about the containment procedures being used to safeguard against accidental release. Some biosecurity experts warn that labs working with the Spanish flu virus are not using the highest containment level, and that a simple accident, such as dropping a test tube, could lead to a lab worker becoming infected, and then spreading the infection outside the lab. During the SARS epidemic of 2003, there were no less than three incidents of accidental release of the virus from labs working at the same containment levels.

Between October 2004 and February 2005, meanwhile, the US government mistakenly sent out thousands of testing kits that contained samples of the 1968 Asian flu. Supposedly all of these were subsequently destroyed, but mistakes such as this raise the prospect that a terrorist organisation could get its hands on a sample. Unlike the better-known bioterror agents, such as anthrax or smallpox, flu would be relatively easy to spread. A terrorist in a major city could infect himself and then spend time in as many crowded places as possible before he become too ill. If he visited an airport, the virus could well be carried round the globe before the authorities even knew there was a threat. A bioterror attack like this might affect everyone on the planet, including those the terrorist believed he was helping through his action – but logic and common sense are not the strong points of extremist fanatics. Most experts in the field, however, believe that a pandemic is much more likely to arise naturally than accidentally or intentionally. According to Professor Oxford, 'Mother Nature has always been the greatest threat – bigger than any bioterrorist.'

Could we contain a pandemic?

The only treatment for flu is anti-viral medicine. This can help to reduce symptoms in those infected and slow the spread of the disease. The best measure, however, is prevention, which can be achieved with a vaccine. A proto-vaccine based on avian flu is already available, but in the event of an outbreak the exact strain must be isolated and analysed so that the proto-vaccine can be modified into the finished article. This must then be mass-produced, distributed around the globe and then administered to as many people as possible – a logistical nightmare.

So the key determinants of how well and how quickly a pandemic could be contained are whether anti-virals and vaccines can be manufactured and distributed quickly enough. This in turn depends on manufacturing capacity and building up stocks pre-emptively. Many of the world's richer countries are already doing this, but even here there is doubt about manufacturing capacity. One of the world's major vaccine makers closed down in 2004, and one of the two main anti-virals is no longer being made – sparking concern amongst experts that if the pandemic came there would not be sufficient capacity. Most agree, however, that capacity could rapidly be expanded, and since the most destructive stage of a pandemic is the second wave of infections – some months after the initial wave – the developed world should be able to marshal its resources in time. The world's poorest countries, on the other hand, will rely on the generosity of richer nations, and are likely to suffer delays that will mean them bearing the brunt of the death toll.

In summary, a pandemic is most likely inevitable at some point in the next few decades, but advances in medicine and public health monitoring (which should give enough warning to allow the authorities to take action) mean that it probably won't be as destructive as the Spanish flu of 1918, and therefore won't threaten civilisation.

Likelihood: 7
Damage: 2
Fear factor: 4

Superbugs

Antibiotics are often lauded as one of the greatest inventions in history – the miracle weapon that allowed mankind to defeat its ancient enemy: the disease-causing bacteria. But their massive and indiscriminate use in medicine, cleaning products, animal feed and even genetic engineering means that we risk creating new strains of superbug – bacteria that are resistant to everything medical science can throw at them, and which will wreak a terrible havoc on future generations.

For many years antibiotics have been prescribed routinely to people who are ill, whether or not their disease will respond. Patients who use antibiotics often do not finish the course and dispose of the medicines carelessly. Antibiotic agents are also used in many cleaning and household products, and antibiotics are added to most animal, poultry and fish feed (not necessarily to fight infections, but because they seem to boost growth). Most bacteria that come into contact with an antibiotic will die, but a few will carry genes that make them resistant to the drug. They will survive and, with all their competition removed, they will flourish. In essence, our massive use of antibiotics is selecting bacteria for antibiotic resistance, causing a sort of forced evolution.

Genes for antibiotic resistance, meanwhile, are essential tools in genetic engineering, used as markers and for helping to select successful gene transfers. In this way they often make their way into genetically modified (GM) species, including GM foods. It is known that bacteria can pick up genes from plants through DNA transfer, so the concern is that by putting resistance genes into GM plants and planting millions of them, we are effectively helping to arm the other side in the long war between us and the bacteria. Once so armed, bacteria can pass on the vital genes to other bacteria, again through DNA transfer.

The upshot is that antibiotic-resistant bacteria are becoming more widespread and more resistant to more types of antibiotic. Probably the best-known form of antibiotic-resistant bacteria is MRSA (which stands for *methicillin-resistant Staphylococcus aureus*). Some strains of MRSA are multi-drug resistant, but at least they are mainly restricted to people in hospitals with weakened immune systems and/or open wounds. A new strain known as Community Acquired (CA) MRSA, however, infects healthy young people in the wider community and can be transferred by simple skin contact. It can cause severe boils and abscesses and even pneumonia that kills within 24 hours. CA-MRSA is not multi-drug resistant, but the nightmare scenario is that it will acquire or evolve multiple resistance, to produce a superbug that combines indestructibility with pandemic prevalence.

What will happen if superbugs become too strong?

We are engaged in a constant arms race with bacteria. As they develop resistance to an antibiotic, our scientists devise new drugs to use against them. But antibiotic development is a slow process, whereas, thanks to human activities such as indiscriminate antibiotic use and genetic modification technology, bacterial evolution of resistance is rapidly accelerating. If a virulent form of multi-drug resistant CA-MRSA developed it could outpace our ability to develop new drugs.

Such a superbug would spread rapidly through human–human contact. At first outbreaks would be centred on places where people are in close contact – gyms and changing rooms, prisons, clubs and bars, public transport, hospitals and schools. The bug would also be passed between family members and friends. Once infected, the victim might develop boils and sores, fever, pneumonia and meningitis. In some cases the immune system would be overcome entirely and the victim would die. Doctors would be powerless to help.

How bad such a pandemic might become or what the death rate would be are impossible to know, but it is easy to envisage a scenario of panic and despair. The authorities would attempt to impose quarantines, but fearful citizens might ignore them and flee affected regions, carrying the killer bugs with them. The streets would be deserted and the cities emptied. The developed world is the most reliant on antibiotics, so it would probably be worst affected, but as with the flu pandemic there could be grim knock-on effects for the world economy and for quality of life for all world citizens.

Has it happened before?

Incurable pandemics were a regular feature of life for most of human history, but they involved germs where drug resistance was not an issue, as it is with modern MRSA (although there is concern about, for instance, drug-resistant tuberculosis). However, there have been precursors to CA-MRSA. It is a strain of the common bacterium *Staphylococcus aureus*, and is probably closely related to a form of penicillin-resistant *Staphylococcus aureus* that caused a global outbreak of infections during the 1950s. Fortunately this early form of superbug wasn't all that super, and an alternative antibiotic, methicillin, was quickly rolled out to bring it under control. Future superbugs may be tougher customers.

How likely is it to happen?

MRSA is already killing around 900 people a year in the UK – the country worst affected – while CA-MRSA has spread throughout the US and has also reached France, Switzerland, Denmark, Saudi Arabia, India, Australia and New Zealand. In some countries the incidence has doubled in the past two years. Eventually it is inevitable that this strain and others will acquire multiple drug resistance, but the real question is how quickly will this happen?

At the moment human ingenuity seems to be up to the challenge posed by superbugs and their gradual development of multiple drug resistance, but will factors such as the increasing prevalence of GM crops accelerate this development, and if so, by how much? These are great unknowns. Optimists might argue that, if a superbug pandemic did break out, the full power of science would be brought to bear on the development of new antibiotics and the disease would quickly be brought under control without threatening civilisation. Pessimists might not be so sure.

Likelihood: 3
Damage: 2
Fear factor: 2

Rogue AI

Since the dawn of the computer age, one of the dreams of computer scientists has been to create an AI comparable to or greater than that of humans. Such an intelligence – equipped with the number-crunching power of a computer, with instant access to all recorded knowledge yet free of the constraints of humanity – would set off a cascade of new technology. It could upgrade itself faster than any human design process could achieve. Society would be transformed. But how could we guarantee that this new intelligence would be benign – that it wouldn't use its power to harm or destroy us?

What will happen if AI gets out of control?

Rogue AI is a staple of science fiction. From the computer HAL of *2001: A Space Odyssey*, to the 'machines' of *The Terminator* and *The Matrix*, science fiction has offered plausible pictures of what might happen if AI goes wrong.

In *2001: A Space Odyssey* (which was written before the advent of the Internet and is therefore missing an element of inter-connectedness) HAL, an AI comparable to a human mind, is housed in a single computer that runs a spaceship. Like a human mind, HAL is capable of going off the rails and does so with homicidal results, using its control over the ship's systems to dispatch several of the crew, supposedly in support of its core programming to ensure the success of the mission. The *Terminator/Matrix* scenario envisages a more connected, grander form of AI, which quickly becomes more intelligent than its human creators and uses the inter-connectedness of global IT to wrest control of major systems. Where necessary, the AI creates robots and other machines to act as proxies in its evil scheme. Civilisation is destroyed through nuclear war and the surviving humans driven into hiding to eke out a hunted existence. The recent film *I, Robot* offers a slightly less apocalyptic scenario; a central computer remotely controls millions of robots and uses them to take over the state, hold humans prisoner and dispose of those who oppose it.

Are these scenarios plausible? A successful AI would probably be housed on some sort of powerful mainframe, with extensive access to the Internet and, through it, to other computers around the world. It would also probably combine intelligence with access to vast processing power and virtually all recorded knowledge, so perhaps it would be capable of hacking into control systems, over-riding security routines and working out passwords. It might even be able to take control of important systems such as water and power supply, transport and, crucially, weapons systems.

An AI could even manipulate the physical world; it could wrest control of remotely controlled robots (eg car-building factory robots), and given enough time it might be able to construct robot factories or self-replicating robots. Sounds far-fetched? One of the tenets of the AI research community is that when AI is finally created, it will act as a catalyst for something known as 'the singularity': a breakthrough moment when technological progress accelerates far beyond what humans have previously been able to achieve or even imagine.

Has it happened before?

Intelligent computers and robots are the stuff of science fiction rather than history, but if they are conceived of as slaves, employees or mercenaries, subject to the will of their owners or masters, a number of parallels for the perils of rogue AI become clear. There have been many slave revolts in history, and also instances where formerly subjugated or servile groups have gained more power than their masters and overthrown them. For instance, the Jutes and Frisians were Saxon tribes who were initially invited to south-east England by Celtic kings as mercenaries during the 5th century, but grew numerous and powerful enough to conquer territory and supplant Celtic culture with their own. The Janissaries were a caste of slaves and prisoners of war forced into military servitude for the Ottomans, but by the early 18th century they virtually ran the Ottoman Empire. Similarly, the Mameluks were slave soldiers who took control of Egypt to rule as their own kingdom. Would a future army of sentient robots or AIs consider themselves slaves and covet a kingdom of their own?

How likely is it to happen?

Grand claims for the imminent arrival of AI have a bad record. When computers were first invented in the 1940s, it was predicted that AI would arrive within decades. During the early 1980s major research programmes funded by the Japanese and US governments created considerable AI hype, with rash predictions about intelligent computers and robots arriving by the early 1990s, but when these claims proved to be groundless the collapse in funding caused an 'AI winter'. AI became almost a dirty word, and many researchers in the field now prefer to restrict their focus to more specific goals, such as voice recognition or visual processing.

Nonetheless, some AI pioneers are still confident enough to

make grandiose predictions. Speaking to *New Scientist* magazine in 2005, Doug Lenat, founder of Cycorp and creator of an AI system called Cyc, claimed, 'We are heading towards a singularity and we will see it in less than 10 years.' Meanwhile in an article in the *Guardian* newspaper, Hans Moravec, AI and robotics pioneer and research professor at Carnegie Mellon University's Robotics Institute in Pittsburgh, argues:

> *Robot controllers double in complexity (processing power) every year or two. They are now barely at the lower range of vertebrate complexity, but should catch up with us within a half-century. By 2050 I predict that there will be robots with humanlike mental power, with the ability to abstract and generalise.*

But most experts are much more circumspect, and the relatively slow pace of progress to date does not inspire confidence in the future of AI or robotics. Perhaps the greatest hurdle is that intelligence itself is a poorly understood/defined concept – perhaps one that can never be adequately explained. Some experts are sceptical that we can even begin to develop successful AI until this hurdle is overcome, while others argue that this will never happen, and that it will be impossible for a machine to ever be intelligent like a human.

Friend or foe?

Even if AI could be achieved, there is no reason to assume that it would be evil/dangerous. For instance, an AI might be programmed with morals and strict fail-safes limiting its power or malice. It might follow a human-like developmental pathway, starting off with an infantile level of intelligence, and learning human emotions such as compassion and love as it 'grew up', just as humans do.

Some philosophers argue that any AI would not want to destroy humanity because it might not actually *want* anything: it might have no desires or intentions. Why should it? Just because humans have desires and intentions, why should artificial intelligence? Not everyone agrees with this line of reasoning, but until AI is achieved no one will really know.

On balance, the danger of a rogue AI destroying civilisation must be reckoned as extremely low. AI could be decades or even centuries away. It might even be impossible to achieve at all. And even if it was created, it would not necessarily be dangerous.

Likelihood: 0.1

Damage: 9

Fear factor: 1

Physics experiment gone wrong

It's the year 1999. President Clinton is alarmed. Reports of a terrible threat emanating from a laboratory on Long Island in New York have prompted him to call for a security briefing. Is it true, he wants to know? Could the Earth be in danger?

Bizarrely this is not fiction. Clinton genuinely did ask for a briefing on goings on at the Brookhaven National Laboratory. But why? The lab is home to the Relativistic Heavy Ion Collider (RHIC), a particle accelerator or 'atom smasher'. Giant magnets accelerate atoms of gold almost to the speed of light, and then smash them into one another. The incredible energies involved shake sub-atomic particles in the nuclei of the gold atoms loose, so that – just for a nanosecond – a few of them dissolve into a new state of matter called a quark-gluon plasma (a plasma is a sort of fireball of super-hot gas). By studying this plasma scientists hope to learn about the basic building blocks of the universe and the conditions that existed at the beginning of time.

In 1999 it was suggested that these atom-smashing experiments could threaten the existence of the planet by either creating a mini-black hole or setting off a chain reaction of 'strange matter' conversion. In the first scenario, the concern was that the powerful collision of the gold atoms would cause the nuclei to merge, forming matter so dense it would generate enough gravity to collapse in on itself as a miniature black hole. The second scenario revolves around an exotic theoretical form of matter known as strange matter, where subatomic particles are made up of more quarks than usual. According to some calculations, there is a chance that the RHIC atom-smashing could result in the creation of a tiny blob of strange matter, called a strangelet. According to other calculations, there is also a chance that if a strangelet came into being, it would 'convert' surrounding conventional particles into more strangelets, setting off a chain reaction.

What will happen if mini-black holes or strangelets are created?

Black holes generate such extreme gravitational forces that they pull in all mass and energy around them, even light. Exactly what happens to this matter and energy isn't clear, but according to the theories of Stephen Hawking, it is converted into a form of energy now known as Hawking radiation. If a mini-black hole were to appear in Long Island, and if it lasted for long enough, it could attract enough mass to sustain itself and grow. Sucking in matter as it went, it would 'fall' through the planet until it reached the centre and then it would suck in the rest of the Earth, and everything on it, in just a few minutes. Civilisation, mankind and all life on Earth would be reduced to a faint glow of Hawking radiation.

In the event of a strangelet chain reaction, all matter on Earth, and possibly in the Universe, would be transformed into a sort of soup or plasma of strange matter, probably within a few instants.

Has it happened before?

Obviously this has not happened within the lifetime of the planet, and (as far as a strangelet chain reaction goes) probably not within the lifetime of the Universe. Similar fears, however, were raised by the pioneers of the atom bomb. Edward Teller, for instance, raised the possibility that a nuclear explosion would produce such high temperatures that the atmosphere itself would be set on fire in a self-sustaining conflagration. Another physicist, Hans Bethe, theoretically proved that this would not happen, but others remained concerned about the possibility until the first test of a nuclear bomb proved it wrong in practice.

How likely is it to happen?

The RHIC atom-smasher produces immensely energetic particles, and is unusual in using gold atoms as the 'bullets' that are fired at one another. Gold atoms are particularly massive, and it is this unusual feature that probably sparked off initial fears about mini-black holes. To add to concerns, recent research suggests that a fireball of plasma created at RHIC did indeed have the characteristics of a black hole. When RHIC creates a fireball, its existence can only be detected indirectly by measuring how many particles it absorbs. When physicist Horatiu Nastase of Brown University in Providence, Rhode Island, looked at one of the fireballs, he found that it absorbed ten times more particles than predicted – as if it were drawing them in like a black hole.

However, while there may be enough suggestive information to generate alarmist headlines, a closer look shows that fears about the Brookhaven Laboratory's experiments are unfounded. The initial comments by scientists that set off the headlines regarded the incredibly minute probability that a doomsday scenario might unfold. In effect, what the scientists were saying was, 'It may not be impossible for this to happen,' which is quite different from saying, 'There is a serious chance of this happening.' Subsequent calculations showed that the energies and mass involved in the RHIC work are not great enough to produce a self-sustaining black hole. Also, even if the RHIC generated millions of times as much energy and a tiny black hole did come into existence, it has been mathematically calculated that the hole would disappear almost instantaneously, rendering it completely harmless. Similarly, the strangelet scenario is considered so astronomically unlikely that it is effectively impossible, as it relies on a series of highly unlikely circumstances and unproven assumptions.

The best reason for not worrying about the Brookhaven experiments, however, comes from space. Some of the showers of particles hurtling through space (known as cosmic rays) are much more energetic than the particles in RHIC, and they regularly smash into other particles, such as those in the Earth's atmosphere or on the surface of the Moon. The Moon sustains billions of atom-smashing events every second – many of which are far more powerful than anything that can be achieved at RHIC – and has done so for billions of years; yet in all the time this natural atom-smashing experiment has been going on, there have been no doomsday consequences. Perhaps in the future a physics experiment of far greater scope and ambition will carry serious risks, but at present there is no cause for concern.

Likelihood: 0.00000001
Damage: 10
Fear factor: 0.0000001

Conclusion: Frankenstein's monster unmasked

The threat of Frankenstein science unleashing Armageddon from the laboratory makes for good headlines and fits in with archetypes such as the mad professor, the dangerous boffin who delves too deep and the arrogant scientist brought low by hubris. Most of all, it plays to our deep-seated anxieties about the overly rapid pace of change, and fear of alienation in an impersonal, technological world. But, as this chapter has shown, none of the threats currently posed by science and technology are likely to bring civilisation crashing down, although a global pandemic could cause great suffering.

This is not to say that science and technology cannot be dangerous or have disastrous unintended consequences –

they certainly have done in the past. Classic examples include the disastrous effects of CFCs on the ozone layer, which probably won't recover until 2050 at the earliest, or the health impact of the discovery that adding lead to petrol helps to prevent engine knock. But the only human technology that genuinely threatens civilisation through unintended consequences (nuclear weapons are *supposed* to be destructive) is probably the internal combustion engine and associated fossil fuel-burning technology, which produce emissions that may result in climate change (covered in chapters 3 and 4). If this chapter has a message, it is that we should concern ourselves with real and immediate threats, such as climate change and environmental crisis, and not worry too much about scenarios with a very low to non-existent probability of happening.

Chapter 2

Third World War

Marco isn't happy. His parents supported the Conscription Bill, but it wasn't them who had to join up. And now after three months of gruelling boot camp he's been shipped out to the Frontier Zone to spend twelve-hour watches sweating in an environmental suit whilst staring out over a blasted wasteland. Out there only lichen can grow, along with the occasional patch of horribly mutated fungus where bones poke out of the rubble. Despite the heat, Marco shivers at the thought of all the unconsecrated mass graves and the hundreds of thousands of shattered, burned bodies lying where they fell, but what really scares him are the fresh burial pits at the foot of the Wall, directly below where he stands guard. Some of the second-tour vets like to tell stories about refugee children dumped in alive along with their dead parents, and what they end up eating if they manage to claw their way to the surface.

Abruptly, Marco is shaken from his grim reverie. The alarm sirens are sounding; something's coming. He soon spots the ragtag crowd of travellers stumbling out of the badlands. How they got past the Internment Zone he doesn't know. Perhaps they didn't; perhaps they broke out of one of the Camps, in which case there could be tens of thousands more on the way. At least that would mean they're less likely to be a suicide squad posing as refugees.

Marco follows procedures and sounds the various warnings, but the group trudges on until they arrive at the foot of the Wall, where they stop and set up an unholy wailing. Marco can't hear what they're saying, and procedures strictly forbid him from going down to find out, but he can pretty much guess from the way the adults are holding up the small bundles that look like rags but for the little feet sticking out. That doesn't mean much – the first thing you learn in basic is that anything can be a bomb. One of the men starts trying to climb the Wall, apparently impervious to the electrified casing. Procedures say that Marco has to open fire, but if he does he'll hit the others. Three months of basic didn't prepare him for this. What's he supposed to do?

A world at war

In this colourful scenario, Marco and the refugees are at the sharp end of a horrible but plausible nexus of social, economic, political and environmental problems, from the pressure of mass immigration and the threat of extremism to the environmental consequences of weapons of mass destruction (WMD) and the pain of global injustice. Could encounters like this become all too common as an overcrowded world struggles to divide up diminishing resources, leading to tension, instability, conflict and outright war? This chapter examines some of the possible scenarios that could lead to conflict on a scale big enough to threaten civilisation as we know it, from the threat of WMD to the perils of fundamentalist extremism.

Apocalypse now?

Ask people today what springs into their mind when they hear the phrase 'doomsday scenario' and they will probably answer 'global warming' or 'asteroid strike'. But these are relatively recent concerns. Fifty years ago the widespread response would have been 'nuclear Armageddon': the use of WMD by warring superpowers engaged in mutually assured destruction. With the end of the Cold War the threat from WMD seemed to have receded, but since the terrorist attacks of 11 September 2001 they are back on the agenda. We are living in a less stable, more dangerous world, where rogue states possess WMD or are attempting to acquire them, and fanatical terrorists seek to do as much damage as possible with any and all means they can get their hands on.

There are two distinct classes of threat from WMD. On the one hand, there is the danger that one state could launch nuclear missiles at another, sparking a nuclear escalation. On the other hand, there is the danger that a group of terrorists could get hold of a WMD device. (This specific terror threat is considered below – see 'Terror unlimited'.)

What will happen if the missiles start flying?

The US and Russia still have enough missiles aimed at each other's major cities to achieve 'mutually assured destruction': the certainty that the majority of the populations of both countries would be killed. The far more likely threat, however, comes from one of the potential flashpoint regions of nuclear tension (as detailed on page 44); in these scenarios there would be fewer, less powerful missiles affecting a smaller region.

For those in the target zone the results of a nuclear missile would be apocalyptic. A nuclear blast generates temperatures of several million ºC – hotter than the surface of the Sun. Within a central zone of total destruction people are simply vaporised by the initial heat flash. Around this zone the heat and blast ignite and flatten both buildings and people, with instantaneous death rates of 90 per cent plus. Although immediate survival rates increase with distance from the blast, injuries tend to be very severe with very low longer term survival rates.

The exact radii of the various zones depend on the megatonnage of the weapon. At Hiroshima, where a comparatively small bomb of 15 kilotons (ie equivalent to 15,000 tonnes of TNT) was used, the zone of total destruction had a radius of about 0.8 kilometre (0.5 mile), and at least 140,000 people were killed within four months of the bomb being dropped. Most nuclear weapons today are hundreds of times more powerful.

Fallout

A wide zone outside the target would be affected by radioactive fallout (radioactive dust and ash blown high into the atmosphere to rain down over large areas). The amount of fallout depends on whether the weapon is set to detonate on impact or above the ground, with the latter throwing up far more debris. The range of the fallout depends on wind and rain; for instance, fallout from the Chernobyl nuclear power station disaster in 1986 fell on North Wales, more than 1,000 miles away.

Exposure to fallout causes radiation sickness, which is untreatable and has a high mortality rate. Even low exposure can kill, and often causes miscarriage, congenital abnormalities and long-term health consequences, such as thyroid cancer and leukaemia. A region devastated by nuclear strikes would remain contaminated for several years afterwards, although the exact length of time depends, again, on the type of bomb used.

Nuclear winter

Though devastating for the target region, the immediate consequences of nuclear blasts might not affect civilisation as a whole. The effects of a nuclear explosion on the atmosphere, however, could threaten the very survival of the human species, through the phenomenon known as 'nuclear winter': a version of global dimming (see Chapter 3) caused by dust and debris from the explosions and smoke and ash from the fires spreading out in the upper atmosphere and screening out solar radiation. This would cause a dramatic cooling of the Earth's surface and would reduce the amount of sunlight below the threshold for plant photosynthesis.

Even a limited nuclear conflict could produce this doomsday outcome. When the astronomer Carl Sagan and his colleagues initially developed the nuclear winter theory in the early 1980s, they calculated that even a relatively small-scale nuclear war, involving 'only' 100 megatons of warheads, would ignite enough fires and raise enough dust to cause cooling of between 5 and 15°C in the Northern Hemisphere.

Subsequent work has suggested that Sagan and his colleagues over-estimated the cooling effects, and that the more likely result would be a 'nuclear autumn'. Even this, however, would severely impact the global ecosystem, damage global agriculture and place massive stress on societies as they struggle to warm and feed their populations.

In addition to this threat, the atmospheric detonation of nuclear devices ('airbursts') would convert nitrogen in the upper atmosphere into nitrogen oxides, which have a destructive effect on the ozone layer. So, once the nuclear winter or autumn cleared, the Earth's surface and the survivors would be exposed to high levels of dangerous UV radiation.

Has it happened before?

The only uses of nuclear devices as weapons of war remain the attacks on Hiroshima and Nagasaki on 6 and 9 August 1945, respectively. Although these involved devices of a smaller magnitude than most current warheads, they bear grim witness to the localised consequences of WMD, which included death tolls of around 300,000 in the short-term and many more over the following decades. Fortunately, there is no parallel to the effects of a large-scale nuclear conflict in human history.

There is, however, a parallel further back in the geological record – namely, the consequences of massive asteroid impacts. The effects of an impact, such as that believed to have finished off the dinosaurs 65 million years ago, were most likely similar to a nuclear winter. The initial impact probably caused enormous firestorms, and the dust, ash, smoke and debris lifted into the atmosphere by the impact and the fires subsequently spread all around the globe. Whether this resulted in a full-blown nuclear winter is a contentious issue, but most scientists believe that a wave of extinctions was set in motion. (See Chapter 5 for more on this.)

How likely is it to happen?

Since 1947 a group of the world's top experts on nuclear weapons and international geopolitics has thoughtfully provided a measure of the likelihood of nuclear Armageddon, in the form of the Doomsday Clock, symbol of the journal *Bulletin of the Atomic Scientists*. The Clock, which features on their cover each issue, graphically depicts their assessment of the risk of nuclear conflict through the proximity of the clock's hands to midnight (which equates to doomsday). In 2002 the Doomsday Clock was reset at seven minutes to midnight, the same as on its debut 58 years ago, the third time the hands have moved forward since the end of the Cold War in 1991. In other words, the people in the know think that the risk of nuclear war is increasing, not receding. How can this be?

Proliferation

The end of the Cold War, together with the apparent success of important treaties such as the Nuclear Non-Proliferation Treaty, the Anti-Ballistic Missile Treaty and others, led to a general expectation that the nuclear threat was over. The warheads, however, remain. The US currently has around 7,000 active warheads and 3,000 reserve warheads in its stockpile, while Russia has around 8,000 active and 10,000 in reserve/awaiting disassembly. The three other traditional nuclear powers, China, France and Britain, have 420, 350 and 200 active warheads respectively. Progress on standing down active weapons and disassembling deactivated ones remains slow.

On the other hand, a number of other states, including Israel, India and Pakistan, have acquired nuclear weapons – they may have more than 350 warheads between them. It is widely suspected that North Korea has already acquired nuclear capability, and that Iran is actively trying to do so and may not be far off.

Flashpoints

There are several parts of the world where regional tension coincides with nuclear capability to create potential nuclear flashpoints.

- *India–Pakistan*: These nations have gone to war several times since they were created after the Second World War, and escalating tension between the two over the Kashmir crisis was one of the main reasons that the *Bulletin* reset their Doomsday Clock in 2002. Today tension in the region has eased, but the potential for conflict remains strong. In particular, the situation in Kashmir remains unresolved, and only a lack of democracy in Pakistan prevents hard-line Islamist parties from taking control of the country and its nuclear arsenal.

- *The Middle East*: The anti-Israeli rhetoric of many Middle Eastern countries remains virulent, while Israel has made no secret of its willingness to launch pre-emptive conventional strikes against states that it fears may be developing nuclear weapons, and indeed did so during the 1980s when it attacked nuclear facilities in Iraq. Should Iran acquire the Bomb – as seems likely – the situation would become very volatile. It is easy to imagine a scenario where Israel launches a pre-emptive strike on what it believes to be a pre-nuclear Iran, only to discover that they already have the Bomb when it is used in retaliation, triggering regional escalation. If Pakistan weighed in to support a fellow Islamic nation, the conflict could escalate still further.

- *China*: There is tension between: China and Taiwan over the latter's claims to independence; China and the US over American support for Taiwan; and China and Japan over territorial and mineral rights in the South China Sea. Recent military exercises by China in the waters off Taiwan have increased tension and prompted an escalation of US forces in the region. Also Sino–Japanese relations have been damaged by an incursion into Japanese waters by a mystery submarine in November 2004, and by recent rows over war guilt and oil rights.

- *North Korea*: One of the world's most autocratic regimes cannot feed its people properly but indulges in constant belligerent rhetoric towards South Korea and the US. Meanwhile its test missile launches over Japan are more than just rhetoric. The lunacy of the North Korean regime makes it unpredictable. For instance, how would it respond to a massive internal crisis brought on by famine, or to a more aggressive stance by the US on nuclear proliferation by rogue states?

- *USA*: The *Bulletin* argues that the actions of the US have had more of a negative impact on the Doomsday Clock than those of rogue states or terrorists. Many commentators feel that aggressive unilateralism by the US is actually stoking the fires of extremism around the world, while the current administration's withdrawal from several international treaties and pursuit of a missile-defence shield creates further global insecurity.

Hopefully all of these regional tensions will be resolved without recourse to violence, but if the environmental and resource problems described in Chapters 3 and 4 get worse, there could be a whole new raft of regional tensions around issues of dwindling resources. For instance, tension over water in East Africa threatens to escalate into conflict, while diminishing oil reserves could exacerbate tensions in the Far and Middle East and Central Asia.

On balance, the threat of all-out nuclear war has probably receded with the end of the Cold War, but the threat of a regional nuclear conflict, with nonetheless terrible global consequences, is quite real.

Likelihood: 2
Damage: 7
Fear factor: 3

Terror unlimited

A single terrorist carrying a suitcase-sized WMD device could destroy an entire city. Could an army of such fanatics bring down civilisation? Prior to the advent of extremist terrorism of the Al Qaeda school, terrorism was political in nature. But the avowed aims of this new brand of terrorist are explicitly apocalyptic. Al Qaeda and associated Islamist terror groups believe in a biblical vision of warring cultures, in which their brand of extreme puritanical Islam does final battle with the forces of evil for control of the Universe. If this means toppling civilisation through indiscriminate terror, so be it. Al Qaeda is not the only group to espouse such a vision.

Extremist cults such as Japan's (now supposedly defunct) Aum Shinrikyo share similar beliefs and have shown that they are willing to attempt to put them into practice.

For many people, warnings about terrorists seeking to lay their hands on WMD have been devalued by their use for political ends by politicians such as George Bush and Tony Blair. But it is a matter of record that terror groups have attempted to acquire WMD, raising the prospect that future terrorist attacks might involve suitcase-sized atomic bombs, dirty bombs (which use conventional explosives to scatter radioactive material), release of disease agents such as plague, anthrax or smallpox, or chemical attack through release of nerve gas or poisoning of water supplies.

What will happen if terrorists do use WMD?

A suitcase-sized atomic bomb could destroy a major city with appalling loss of life. In theory a well-placed and timed dirty bomb could kill thousands directly through radiation poisoning, create widespread panic and lead to the shut-down of a city centre, possibly for years. In practice, however, nobody really knows how dangerous such a device would be because no one has ever let one off. However, in 1987, during the Iran–Iraq war, the Iraqis did test such a device, concluding that it would not be worthwhile because of the low level of radiation produced, so a dirty bomb may not be quite as terrible as is feared.

Biological agents, such as anthrax spores or smallpox virus, could have horrible consequences, but in practice they are considered a relatively low-risk threat because of the difficulties involved in dispersal. Advanced technology is needed to spray or otherwise disperse the agents in such a fashion that they actually spread from the point of release. Similar problems apply to nerve gas. This is illustrated by the comparatively low toll of the 1995 Tokyo subway gas attack by Aum Shinrikyo. The deadly nerve agent sarin was released into a crowded subway, and although 5,000 people were hospitalised only 12 died. While undoubtedly a terrible tragedy for those involved, this obviously does not constitute a threat to civilisation. Contamination of municipal water supplies with an agent such as ricin – apparently the intent of an Islamic extremist plot recently foiled by British police – might be a more effective and thus dangerous way to use chemical agents.

In all these instances it seems unlikely that a successful attack would actually threaten civilisation. However, there are some plausible doomsday scenarios. An attack on one of the centres of global wealth – New York, Tokyo or London – could potentially devastate the global economy through a ripple effect. The confidence that sustains global markets could be undermined, causing a global crash, while the damage to institutions and records would undermine the system itself. The sheer loss of capital would also contribute to a global crash. Once a negative spiral sets in, there could be a savage global depression worse than the Great Depression of the 1930s. Would this constitute a threat to civilisation?

What if terrorists become more sophisticated and powerful than today, and were able to launch multiple attacks? Suitcase atomic bombs in all of the world's major cities, or well-coordinated release of a specially selected transgenic avian flu virus (see 'Pandemic', page 14) in a dozen densely populated countries would, at the very least, shake the foundations of civilisation. Perhaps the most worrying threat, however, is that a terrorist outrage could spark off a wider war.

After 9/11, for instance, many American voices were raised in support of a nuclear strike against regimes that supposedly backed the attack. What if 9/11 had involved nuclear weapons? If Iranian-sponsored terrorists let off a nuclear device in Israel, would Israel respond by launching a strike on Iran? Terrorists might achieve their wish and provoke Armageddon.

Has it happened before?

Fortunately there has never been a terror strike of the magnitude under discussion here. But history provides a chilling example of how a small group of dangerous fanatics can touch off a global conflagration. In the early 20th century the statesmen of the Great Powers of Europe assumed that their carefully balanced system of treaties would keep the peace and head off large-scale wars, but their calculations did not take into account the impact of the growing tide of extremist nationalistic fervour in many parts of the continent. This tide reached its peak in the Balkans, where a gang of extreme Serbian nationalists assassinated Austrian Archduke Franz Ferdinand. Austria promptly declared war on Serbia, but the complex series of treaties meant that in doing so they dragged Russia, Britain, France and Germany into war as well. What would the outcome have been if nuclear weapons had existed then?

How likely is it to happen?

Building WMD requires expertise, technology and exotic materials. It is difficult for states to accomplish, so it should be nearly impossible for terrorists. But not actually impossible. Most security analysts rule out the possibility of terrorists devising a suitcase atomic bomb of their own, but there's always the prospect that a disgruntled 'rogue' state could build one for them. For instance, Iran, the country currently in the centre of a dispute over attempts to develop nuclear weapons, is a known sponsor of terrorism. It's conceivable that they might supply a nuclear weapon to a terror group active in Israel as a way of striking at a hated enemy otherwise beyond their reach.

Alternatively terrorists could steal a nuclear device. There are thousands of redundant nuclear devices in the territories of the former Soviet Union, and there is a high level of concern about the security surrounding them. The US is supposedly funding the decommissioning of ex-Soviet devices, but experts warn that this funding amounts to less than a third of the amount necessary. According to the *Bulletin of the Atomic Scientists*, 'It is now essentially impossible to verify whether all materials in the United States and Russia are accounted for or whether all weapons are secure.'

A third option for terrorists would be a cyber-attack on the nuclear power plants or weapons of a target nation. The fail-safe systems that prevent nuclear accidents are computer-controlled, so there is the possibility that skilled hackers could wreak havoc. This scenario formed the plot of a recent series of the US TV drama *24*. While experts dismissed the fictional version as far-fetched, they warn that there is a real risk from hacking.

The most realistic 'nuclear' threat is considered to be a dirty bomb. No new technology would be involved, in making one, and radioactive material may be disturbingly easy to acquire. Since 1993, there have been 630 confirmed incidents of trafficking in radioactive materials; how many more were not detected? Only 18 of these involved weapons-grade material, but for a dirty bomb even low-grade material might be suitable. There are similar security fears over biological and chemical weapons materials. Incidents such as the Aum Shinrikyo attacks or the 2001 anthrax letter scares in the US show that terrorists can either acquire or make such materials.

In summary, the threat from terrorists armed with WMD-related devices is real. However, a combination of the logistical and technological difficulties involved and the vigilance of security agencies makes an actual attack unlikely, and a civilisation-threatening string of attacks extremely implausible.

Likelihood: 4

Damage: 1

Fear factor: 2

Extremism and fundamentalism

What would happen if fanatical extremists were not simply hunted terrorists, but the rulers of powerful nations equipped with nuclear weapons? It might sound like a far-fetched scenario, but there are several reasons to think it could happen. Fundamentalism and nationalism are both growing movements, and extremists of either type could plausibly come to power in countries as potentially danger-ous as Pakistan, Saudi Arabia, the Central Asian republics, India, Egypt, Israel and even the US.

What will happen if extremists come to power?

During the Cold War the deterrent logic of the futility of mutually assured destruction helped to keep the peace and avert the danger of nuclear war. But extremists follow a different brand of logic: one that says, for instance, that indiscriminate destruction is justified by certain ends, or that martyrdom is not to be feared as it leads directly to heaven. In the eyes of such twisted worldviews, nuclear Armageddon might be something to encourage, not avoid.

An easy to imagine scenario sees extremists coming to power in Pakistan, after increasing unrest amongst the people forces current President Musharraf to allow democratic elections. Hardline Islamist parties sweep to power, their share of the vote boosted by anger over recent incidents in Kashmir, and by proof of American misdeeds in Afghanistan. The new Islamist regime threatens both India and Israel with newly developed long-range missiles that can carry nuclear warheads. As tension mounts, fear drives Israelis to elect hardline right-wing Jewish parties to government. India allows Israeli warplanes to set up shop at a base near the disputed Kashmir region, and a local Islamic group attempts to storm the base. Fierce fighting spills over into Kashmir. Pakistan mobilises its nuclear forces, prompting the Israeli warplanes to launch a pre-emptive strike on the Pakistani missile sites. The tension erupts into all-out war and the missiles begin to fly. Large portions of the Middle East and South Asia are devastated and the ensuing environmental crisis creates a global nuclear autumn.

Has it happened before?

Only in recent times has 'enlightened' government become the dominant mode in world politics. For most of history, governments, leaders and peoples have held beliefs that today might be characterised as extremist or fundamentalist. As a result, bloody and destructive wars have characterised most of human history, from the Crusades to the Wars of Religion to World War II. The extent of destruction has only been limited by the available technology.

How likely is it to happen?

Although extremists themselves are not rational or justified, there are reasons why people become extremists. Many commentators argue that US hegemony and unilateralism, combined with increasing global poverty and inequality, are causing resentment, powerlessness and alienation on a global scale, creating fertile ground for extremist ideologies.

In particular, there are several states where extremists could plausibly gain disturbing power. In Pakistan, Saudi Arabia, Egypt and many Central and South East Asian nations, factors such as despotic regimes, crushing poverty and injustice, and heavily funded extremist groups – which are tolerated because they divert disenchantment towards external targets (ie Jews and the US) – have combined to create widespread Islamist movements. These movements are not homogenous, but they do include many extremist groups who openly espouse the creation of pan-Islamic megastates for the purpose of aggressively spreading their brand of fundamentalist religion. Many of these countries possess powerful militaries

(Egypt and Saudi Arabia), or both a powerful military and nuclear capability (Pakistan).

Three other countries that also combine military might with nuclear capability are Israel, India and the US. In all three, there are elected politicians with religious views that might be described as extremist. In Israel, for instance, ultra-conservative religious parties have held the balance of power in recent coalition governments. In India, the electoral success of right-wing Hindu nationalists helped to increase tension with Pakistan and bring the countries to the brink of war. In the US, the key power base of the Bush administration has been fundamentalist Christians. Among the Christian groups that helped to get George W Bush the nomination in the first place are many with close ties to Biblical Reconstructionists. This brand of fundamentalism holds that the Bible is literally true, that the world needs to prepare for the Second Coming by triggering the Apocalypse, and that the Holy Land should be ethnically cleansed of the Palestinians.

In the short-term, the likelihood of any of these countries falling to extremists may be fairly low, but the longer-term picture might not be so rosy. If the predictions of Chapters 3 and 4 prove to be accurate, the world will be faced with tough times: massive poverty, widespread famine and huge population movements. Unfortunately the natural response of most societies to adversity has been the rise of extremism, so the future may belong to the lunatic fringe for whom nuclear weapons are no deterrent.

Likelihood: 2
Damage: 7
Fear factor: 3

Mass migrations

Current levels of immigration are causing great concern in many countries, with unpleasant consequences – racism, violence and reactionary laws. Within a few decades, however, this issue may have grown into a monster that tears our societies apart; for the inevitable consequence of many of the doomsday scenarios in this book will be migrations on a scale unparalleled in human history. Growing populations combined with plummeting standards of living and widespread lack of food security, verging on massive famine, could drive tens or even hundreds of millions of desperate people with nothing to lose to seek succour in the apparent plenty of the developed nations. How would these societies respond to this kind of pressure? Would basic values survive?

What will happen if there are massive migrations?

People who are worried about current levels of immigration warn of many negative impacts. They claim that large influxes over short periods of time lead to ghettoisation, failure to integrate into the host society, insularity and cultural isolation, and thus cultural clashes. The fear is that eventually the host culture itself is changed. There are also concerns about public health issues, with immigrants having higher rates of diseases such as tuberculosis, and a wider fear that letting 'too many' people into the country will inevitably lower living standards for everyone, as the same size cake is divided into smaller and smaller portions. If immigration pressure was to increase massively in the space of a few decades, all of these fears would be magnified accordingly.

Whether these fears are justified or are the product of ignorance and prejudice, they produce a response in host societies, a response that will also be magnified if immigration increases massively. Public fear of being 'swamped' offers fertile ground to populist demagogues and right-wing ideologies, and even if governments are able to resist these influences, they must inevitably respond by hardening their immigration policies.

In a worst-case scenario, developed countries would acquire fortress mentalities, with militarised border controls, extreme border defences (such as walls, protected zones, perhaps even minefields) and harsh treatment of migrants (such as massive detention camps or even forceful military responses). The migrants themselves would suffer a harsh lot. Driven from their homes by desperate conditions, grinding poverty and incipient famine, and having endured arduous and dangerous journeys, they would be faced with hostility, violence and injustice. Within the host countries, anti-immigrant resentment would lead to vigilantism, ethnic tension and violence. It could even spill into race wars as racial hatreds are stirred up. Civilisation as we know it would be radically altered.

Has it happened before?

Mass population movement has been one of the driving forces of human history. Within Europe, for instance, environmental changes, mainly driven by climatic variation, led to population movements such as the invasion of Bronze Age Greece by the Dorians, the assault on ancient Egypt by the Sea Peoples and the European spread of the Celts. Perhaps the most vivid ancient example of the impact of mass population movement on civilisation is the decline of the Western Roman Empire. Climatic variations in the Western Empire weakened Roman hegemony (see page 153), but at the same time population movements from Central Asia and Eastern Europe set off a domino effect of other population movements, which eventually saw Visigoths, Huns and Vandals battering down the gates of Rome and despoiling the Western Empire.

More recent mass migrations had similarly dire effects on the 'host' populations. During the 19th and early 20th centuries, many countries that are now centres of immigration were centres of emigration, as rapid population growth created a damaging disparity between resources and demand. Millions of people, including entire communities, from Ireland, Britain, Germany, Scandinavia and Eastern Europe, transplanted themselves to the 'wide open spaces' of the New World. What happened as a result stands as a grim warning from history. The immigrants came into conflict with indigenous populations – Native Americans, Aztecs and Inca in the Americas, Aborigines in Australia, Maori in New Zealand, Zulu and other tribes in South Africa – causing epidemics, race wars and genocide.

How likely is it to happen?

Many right-wing politicians argue that it already is happening, claiming that immigration to the developed world is getting out of hand. Immigration has been a major issue in several recent election campaigns in countries including the UK, Holland, Australia and Austria, and reactionary responses have increasingly become part of mainstream political debate.

The darker manifestations of anti-immigration reaction are also already to be found. Immigration across the US–Mexican border has reached such high levels (in 2004, along a 260-mile stretch of the Arizona border, the US Border Patrol caught 1,260 people a *day* trying to cross illegally) that far-right militia have mobilised to try to stop it with vigilante action. This vigilante mob, which has dubbed its campaign the Minuteman Project, numbers more than 1,000 members, and is accused of having links with white supremacist and other race-hate organisations. In response, a major Hispanic gang in the US has threatened to 'teach a lesson' to the Minuteman volunteers.

Is this a sign of things to come, with violent vigilante action and the seeds of a race war? That depends on whether the current stream of immigrants becomes a flood. (This, in turn, depends on the likelihood of some of the doomsday scenarios covered in other chapters.) Proponents of unfettered economic growth argue that only by increasing wealth in less developed countries can we make people want to stay at home; but the gloomier view says that this pursuit of growth will lead to destruction of the environment (see 'The aspiration bomb', page 134), and that developing nations will become increasingly unable to support their growing populations as the ecosystem degrades. In this case the poor and huddled masses *will* become an overwhelming tide, because in an era of globalisation and relatively easy international travel, problems from 'over there' will inevitably arrive at our doorstep.

Likelihood: 5

Damage: 3

Fear factor: 4

Conclusion: Peace for our time

Historians still debate whether the deterrent aspect of nuclear weapons helped to avert a third world war in the 20th century. The threat of a world war has probably now receded, but with it has gone any chance of a globally active deterrent. The absence of opposed monolithic power blocs reduces the risk of a global confrontation, but also removes the ability to control aggression or conflict from a central command.

If a future of ecological stress does indeed lead to an erosion of values and an increase in extremism and desperation, there will be a greater likelihood of regional flare-ups but less chance that they can be doused before they burn out of control. Many of the scenarios in this chapter could then come to pass, with mass population movements and bitter resource wars fanning the flames of extremism and stimulating conflict and violence. Putting probabilities to this grim scenario is difficult, because the chances of it becoming reality are dependent on other scenarios, which themselves are not inevitable. The scores assigned to each article in the chapter should be viewed in this context. Ultimately, the degree of optimism or pessimism you feel about prospects for a peaceful future must depend on your assessment of the danger of ecological meltdown and/or catastrophic climate change, the topic of the next two chapters. If you fear the worst for the ecosystem, which on the evidence of Chapters 3 and 4 is very likely, you should also fear a future of conflict.

Chapter 3
Ecocide

Imagine a barren, almost lifeless landscape. A few stunted strands of withered weed struggle out from beneath a choking layer of toxic dust, only to be swallowed by a huge billowing wall of dust as a vast storm rages unchecked across the land, finally blowing itself out far over the ocean. The settling dust blankets a sterile ocean where the only moving things are matted, rotting rafts of garbage hundreds of miles across. Between the rafts the ocean is discoloured by blooms of lurid algae, which form a toxic tide that laps against the tattered shores of a smog-choked city. Rats, mottled and misshapen with tumours and other diseases, root among piles of garbage and try to avoid the traps and snares of the city's few remaining inhabitants – those too weak to trek out to the security zones in the hills and too poor to afford the scant fare available there anyway.

As a stinging acidic rain begins to fall, the outcasts put out containers to gather the toxic fluid, knowing that there is no alternative. Those unlucky enough to be caught out in the badlands scurry to higher ground as the downpour pools on the dusty but unabsorbent ground and gathers into sheets and rivers of mud, scouring the crumbling earth down to the bare bedrock. As night falls the rain stops and another dust storm blows in from far away, obscuring the stars. The inhabitants of the city sit around garbage fires, struggling for warmth, coughing and scratching and trying to ignore their bleeding gums and open sores.

From her vantage point high in a protective dome, hidden behind the fences, wire and guards of the security zone, a high-status woman, one of the fortunate few, peers through the storm searching for any sign of life – a bird or insect, or even just a stray leaf. Finding none, she takes a deep breath of the dry, filtered air, sips her filtered water and toys listlessly with her generic protein gruel. Soon the child will be born and she will dare to leave the safety of the dome for the first time in nine months. How many years will it be until her son can do the same? Will he survive until then, and will there be anything for him to see out there except for the dust, the strangled weeds and the lurid, empty ocean?

Environmental doomsday

This alarming account describes the terrible consequences of ecocide: total meltdown of the global ecosystem as a result of human activities. It probably sounds familiar from a hundred different science fiction books and movies, but this post-apocalyptic scenario could be horribly close to reality.

Is mankind engaged in ecocide? Many concerned environmentalists certainly think so. They warn that human activities are recklessly over-exploiting or degrading almost every aspect of the ecosystem, from the water, air and soil to the plants and animals that live in them, and that sooner or later we will pay the price as the ecosystem collapses and civilisation crumbles. Are they right and if so which will it be – sooner or later? This chapter looks at the disturbing mass of evidence that the doom-mongers are correct, and that ecological meltdown is the most immediate and most serious threat facing civilisation.

What could cause ecocide?

In fact ecocide isn't simply a single threat. It involves many distinct but closely related environmental issues, each of which on its own threatens to, at the every least, severely compromise the quality of life for all world citizens, and each of which should be taken very seriously. The main issues are: pollution; the toxic time bomb of persistent chemicals; the prospect of a hydroxyl holocaust; a water crisis that will leave the Earth parched and mankind gasping for water; a food crisis that could lead to global famine; the threat to wild habitats and species that could destroy the intricate web of life; and the overarching problem of the unsustainable growth of an increasing, and increasingly demanding, global population.

These are issues that have contributed to the failure of past civilisations, but which now, in an era of globalisation, threaten mankind on a scale that is far larger and far more dangerous than anything that has gone before. Each of these issues affects the others in direct and indirect ways. I will explain some of these links as I go along, and will tie them all together at the end of the chapter to show why the apocalyptic account that opens this chapter may not be simply science fiction.

Poisoning the planet

Mankind produces a huge and ever-growing tide of pollution that threatens to poison the air we breathe, the water we drink and the soil in which we grow our crops. In the developed world we are insulated from the true scale of the problem, partly because a lot of pollution is invisible, and partly because most of the worst polluting takes place in the developing world. The range of sources and types of pollution is staggering. If current levels of pollution continue the global ecosystem will gradually degrade. If levels of pollution increase this degradation could be accelerated or there could even be a sudden and catastrophic collapse of the ecosystem.

What will happen if we poison the planet?

The possible consequences of pollution are as varied as its causes. Most of them are issues that already affect large swathes of the global population, but they may get worse, operate on a larger scale or start to seriously damage the quality of life of all world citizens, even those in the relatively sheltered developed world.

To fully understand the potential future impact of pollution you need to appreciate the scale of the existing problems. Water, air and soil pollution already kill millions of people a year.

Water

Water pollution is one of the world's biggest killers, in the form of bacteria, viruses, parasites and other pathogens found in dirty water. Diseases carried in water cause 80 per cent of illness and death in the developing world. Water-mediated diarrhoeal diseases alone kill 2.1 million people per year.

Water can also become contaminated with toxic substances. Falling rain picks up air pollution and dissolves soil pollution, as does water already in the ground. Contaminants can be leached out of rocks and soil from naturally occuring sources or from agricultural, industrial or human sources. Eventually this contaminated water feeds into streams, rivers and underground aquifers, which are then tapped to provide water for drinking, irrigation and for livestock. This means that whatever contaminates groundwater may enter our bodies directly or through the food chain.

A particularly serious example is arsenic contamination of groundwater in Bangladesh. The arsenic exists naturally in rocks below the soil, but the sinking of numerous bore holes for irrigation and drinking water has dramatically increased the rate of contamination. The result is that arsenic levels in some crops that are grown using the contaminated water are as high as 150 parts per million (as opposed to a 'safe' level of 0.01 part per million). The WHO estimates that over the next decade up to 270,000 Bangladeshis will die as a result. This is just one example of the contamination threat facing the world's increasingly stressed water resources. Other types of contamination include heavy metals leached out of mine tailings and organic poisons leached out of landfill sites.

Air

Air pollution exposes humans to toxic chemicals and contributes to a variety of diseases from cancer and emphysema to asthma and allergies. It can even damage the unborn child. According to the WHO, particulates (toxic particles similar to soot) can get into and damage the lungs of babies in the womb. The WHO also reports that each year 3 million people are killed worldwide by outdoor air pollution from vehicles and industrial emissions, and 1.6 million by indoor pollution through using solid fuel. Most are in poor countries, but even air pollution in the US is responsible, by a conservative estimate, for more than 130,000 deaths per year.

Major causes of air pollution include dirty power generation, vehicle fumes and cooking fires. For instance, China's dirty energy industry kills 400,000 people a year through air pollution, incurring annual health costs of $25 billion (and that's just according to official figures). Vehicles produce nitrogen oxides, sulphur dioxide, carbon monoxide, ozone, benzene, lead and many other dangerous substances, including, most harmfully, particulates. Traffic fumes are linked with asthma, cancer, lung disease and even DNA damage. According to one estimate, they kill 20,000 people a year in Europe – more than twice as many as road accidents. In the developed world it may seem difficult to believe that cooking fires can be a real health issue, but for billions in the developing world there is no alternative to burning wood or dung for energy. The fires have a deadly toll; according to the UN Environment programme, cooking fires are responsible for 5 per cent of the world's disease (more than HIV/AIDS) and cost the world around $700 billion a year in lost productivity.

Soil
Soil pollution threatens human health when people farm or build on contaminated land and are thereby exposed to toxic chemicals. Soil contamination can last for centuries, posing an ongoing threat to human health, unless huge sums of money are spent on cleaning it up.

The upshot of all of this is that pollution already kills millions, degrades quality of life for hundreds of millions, and costs the world economy billions in lost productivity. It is damaging civilisation in the Third World in the sense that it retards economic and social development, and if it gets worse it could undo generations of improvements in health and life expectancy. For the developed world the health threat is more insidious, but potentially just as deadly (see 'Toxic time bomb', below).

Dead zones

Water pollution is causing the appearance of huge barren patches in the ocean where nothing survives: dead zones. The mechanism behind these dead zones is called eutrophication. Eutrophication is the technical term for the ageing of an aquatic ecosystem, characterised by a build up of nutrients such as phosphorous and nitrogen that encourages the growth of algae, bacteria and other microscopic life forms. It is a natural process in small bodies of water or where there is little movement of water, but thanks to massive pollution from human activities it has become widespread in the seas and oceans of the world.

Vast quantities of nutrients are washed into the sea by agricultural run-off that is rich in fertilisers, waste from livestock and particularly aquaculture, human sewage, and massive sediment run-off caused by deforestation and ground clearing (which expose soil to erosion so it ends up in the sea). These nutrients then trigger the explosive growth of microorganisms to give what are known as blooms.

Such blooms blanket the sea, blocking sunlight used by photosynthetic organisms and using up all available oxygen, suffocating all other forms of life. Many of the bloom organisms are themselves toxic, resulting in dangerous 'red tides' (the colour is caused by the pigmented algae) that poison fish and humans alike. In China, for instance, red tides affect 75 per cent of lakes and nearly 100 per cent of coastal waters, and have increased in frequency from 5 per year in the 1960s to 100 per year today. The end result of blooms is to create 'dead zones' in the sea, barren marine deserts almost devoid of life. The most famous of these is the dead zone of the Gulf of Mexico, a permanent feature caused by the massive pollution pumped into the Gulf by the Mississippi River. The Gulf dead zone covers up to 15,000 square kilometres, (5,800 square miles).

Dead zones badly stress the already overstretched marine environment, often affecting regions that rely most heavily on the sea for sustenance. If pollution continues to worsen, entire continental coastlines could become dead zones, where toxic tides wash ashore on barren beaches closed off to humans, and fishing fleets sit idle in port as marine foods vanish from the human diet.

Recent research suggests that eutrophic blooms could pose a hitherto unsuspected danger. A 2004 study linked an Alzheimer's-like disease found in inhabitants of the Pacific island of Guam to a neurotoxin produced by cyanobacteria (a type of photosynthetic bacteria often found in eutrophic blooms), which had got into the food chain. This raises the disturbing possibility that similar neurodegenerative diseases and other effects could become more widespread as eutrophic blooms become more widespread and the toxins they produce accumulate in the food chain. For instance, cyanobacteria expert Hans Paerl of the University of North Carolina in Chapel Hill links the growing incidence of liver cancer in parts of China to worsening cyanobacterial contamination of Chinese rivers triggered by agricultural runoff.

Acid rain

During the 1980s, before climate change issues came to dominate the environmental agenda, acid rain was headline news. Today this issue has largely disappeared from view, but the problem itself has not gone away. Acid rain is rain with high levels of dissolved atmospheric gases such as sulphur dioxide or nitrogen oxides. In solution these gases become sulphuric or nitric acid, so the resulting rain is strongly acidic, which has adverse consequences for wildlife, plants and buildings. Water and soil are acidified; trees sicken and die; fish, amphibians and invertebrates die off; and buildings and infrastructure are eroded.

The major sources of the gases that cause acid rain are emissions from power stations, industry, fires (including cooking, forest and coal fires) and vehicles. Although much progress has been made in the developed world in respect of industrial emissions, especially in reducing sulphur dioxide, this good work may be undone by the growth in vehicle emissions, industrial emissions in the developing world and incidence of fires. Even if acidifying gases are brought under control, this will take decades – by which time many ecosystems will already have sustained massive damage.

Dimming and drought

A striking example of the interconnectedness of different environmental and human threats to civilisation is the link between air pollution and disastrous changes in rainfall patterns. Recent modelling at the Australian national research agency, the Commonwealth Scientific and Industrial Research Organisation, suggests that massive emissions of sulphur dioxide by North America and Europe during the 1960s and 70s changed the pattern of heat and therefore rainfall distribution in the Earth's atmosphere. In the northern hemisphere, aerosols (clouds of suspended particles) of sulphate molecules acted as nuclei for droplet formation, producing clouds with lots of small droplets, which were more reflective to solar radiation – a phenomenon known as *dimming*, because it reduces the amount of sunlight reaching the surface. This dimming cooled the northern hemisphere relative to the southern, causing the tropical rainfall belt to shift south, resulting in turn in repeated, catastrophic droughts in sub-Saharan Africa. These were the cause of the terrible famines of the 1970s and 80s. Although reduced sulphur dioxide emissions by the developed world mean that the sub-Saharan droughts have become less severe in recent years, there is disturbing evidence that the process is repeating in Asia. Emissions there are rocketing and changes in rainfall have already been noticed, with persistent droughts in northern China and catastrophic flooding in southern China. So worsening pollution in Asia could threaten the basis of agriculture for the entire region, leading to massive shortfalls in food production together with widespread natural disasters such as flooding and drought.

Poisonous dust storms

Acid rain and sulphur-aerosol related drought are examples of how the less developed world has reaped some of the damage sown by the pollution emitted by the developed world. In recent years the pendulum has started to swing the other way, with pollution from the developing world starting to impact on the (now relatively clean) developed world. An important and worsening example of this is the phenomenon of trans-Pacific dust transport. Huge clouds of pollution form over Asia, made up of vehicle, industrial and domestic emissions, smoke from coal and forest fires, and dust, sand and soil stripped from the landscape at accelerating rates (due to deforestation and other soil problems) and whipped up into massive dust storms by strong winds (themselves partly the result of climate change). The dust and pollution is swept high enough into the atmosphere to get into the jet stream and be carried halfway around the globe before raining down on North America. Amongst this fallout can be found particulates and other toxic substances such as heavy metals. If pollution in Asia worsens (as it is likely to do), and climate change produces more storms and stronger winds (as it is likely to do), this will become an increasingly serious problem for North America, with major health impacts.

Drowning in garbage

A consumer society is predicated on the production of waste. If things aren't thrown away, more things will not be 'consumed' (ie bought to replace them). But the spread of the consumer society to all corners of the globe means that every country will soon share the waste disposal problems of the developed world, where waste is produced at the rate of two tonnes per person per year.

This waste produces a multitude of problems. It takes up space, often where this is at a premium. As it rots it generates methane, making refuse a significant contributor to greenhouse gas emissions. It poses a range of health hazards through spreading dirt and germs, providing pooling spots for stagnant water where mosquitoes can breed (a phenomenon partly blamed for the increasing global incidence of malaria) and leaching toxic substances such as metals and organic chemicals into soil and water. It harms wildlife that eats or is entrapped by it, especially by plastic rubbish. This is a particular problem with refuse that is not confined to landfills. Such garbage is accumulating in the environment at ever increasing rates. For instance, a recent survey of beaches in the UK, where measures are supposedly in place to safeguard the environment, found that there was one piece of litter for every 50 centimetres of coastline (60 per cent of which was plastic litter), and that litter levels had gone up by 82 per cent between 1994 and 2004. Even on remote and uninhabited atolls in the midst of the Pacific Ocean garbage washes up at a density of roughly one piece of litter per metre. Perhaps this is not so surprising, given that the amount of rubbish dumped into the ocean each year is three times greater than the weight of fish caught.

The nature of waste is also changing. Whereas in the past most waste consisted of natural products such as paper, wood and fabrics, which degrade in a relatively benign fashion, an increasing amount of garbage is plastic or hi-tech waste. These types of waste degrade to give toxic chemicals that threaten the health of the nation, and it is almost impossible to dispose of them in such a way as to avoid this.

If waste generation is not somehow reined in, we will find ourselves drowning in a rising tide of garbage, much of it toxic.

Has it happened before?

Past societies probably did suffer greatly from pollution – in particular the health consequences of a poor or non-existent public hygiene infrastructure – but it doesn't seem to have destroyed any of them. The possible exception to this is the medieval Khmer civilisation centred in Angkor, in modern-day Cambodia, which collapsed during the 15th century. Angkor depended on a complex series of canals to irrigate its crops and water its population, and there is some evidence that the decline and fall of the city-state was linked to waste disposal problems, with the canals becoming choked and sewage spreading disease.

On the whole, however, pollution has not been a serious threat to past societies because of the issue of scale. Pollution could be dumped into rivers and from there into the apparently bottomless ocean, or polluting industries could be moved further away. If pollution got really bad, people could simply move on. Even when pollution started to become a problem on an industrial scale, with rapid urbanisation and poorly regulated industries exposing millions of urban poor to fumes, dirt and garbage with disastrous consequences for health, similar solutions prevailed. Industry was moved out of the developed world to the developing world while garbage was simply disposed of away from cities.

But the scale of pollution is now global, and there is no longer any room for manoeuvre. This is what is truly scary about the pollution threat: it is unprecedented in human history. We simply do not know for sure how much rubbish can be poured into the oceans, or what level of fumes the atmosphere can absorb.

How likely is it to happen?

We've already looked at the parlous current state of many forms of pollution. But will pollution worsen to the point that humans, animals and plants are poisoned and the planet is afflicted with acid rain, pollution-triggered droughts, poisonous dust storms and mountains of rubbish?

People living in the developed world can easily be lulled into a sense of false security about pollution, based on the pronouncements of industry and governments about anti-pollution initiatives and clean-up efforts. It is certainly true that some good work has been done – for instance, in the US the levels of six of the major atmospheric pollutants have been slashed over the last few decades. In fact most developed world cities have seen improvements in air and water quality since the 1960s and 70s. However, there are several major reasons for pessimism: cleaning up pollution is expensive, there is poor regulation in the developing world, and the major sources of pollution are getting worse.

Corporate clean up

Some forms of contamination – such as acid leaching (where rainwater drips through mining debris with a high sulphur content, resulting in sulphuric acid runoff) or radioactive waste dumped into the North Sea by British nuclear operations – cannot be cleaned up and will continue to cause pollution for thousands of years. Others can be cleaned up if enough money is spent, but herein lies the problem: who is going to pay? It is in the financial interest of industrial corporations to avoid paying massive clean-up costs, so they use a variety of means to do so. These include:

using financial muscle to lobby politicians to keep regulation loose, declaring bankruptcy after transferring assets to different companies, or simply reneging on promises/breaking the law, in the knowledge that fines will be small in comparison to clean-up costs. All this is common practice in the developed world, let alone in the Third World, where industrial pollution is much worse. If developed countries struggle to make corporations accountable for industrial pollution, how will the problem be brought under control in the Third World?

Anything goes

Corporate accountability is just one of the issues surrounding pollution in the developing world. In general there are less strict regulations, less enforcement and greater corruption in the developing world, with the result that massive pollution goes unchecked and, as industrial development accelerates, will probably get worse.

Another source of problems is export of waste from the developed to the developing world. For instance, much of the hazardous hi-tech waste produced in the developed world is exported to Third World countries, mainly in Asia. According to one report, 50–80 per cent of E-waste (hi-tech waste produced by discarding electronic products such as computers, mobile phones, refrigerators and televisions) that is collected for 'recycling' in the US is immediately shipped out to Asia. Once there it is either dumped or broken up by unprotected, untrained workers who are exposed to the toxic waste and suffer a range of severe health problems as a result. There have been some international efforts to stamp out the pernicious trade, but the main producer of E-waste, the US, has worked hard to undermine them. Similar issues surround the dumping of obsolete toxic pesticides, often long-banned in their countries of origin, in Third World countries. According to the Food and Agriculture Organisation, over 100,000 tonnes of old, toxic pesticides, such as DDT, have been abandoned in Africa and the Middle East, to leak out of corroding drums and into the environment, causing health problems in local populations.

Accelerating pollution

Many of the major sources of pollution are set to become bigger problems in the future, as global economic development continues to accelerate. Economic development usually means more pollution, as more power is needed, more goods and people are transported and more things are bought and thrown away. Three of the biggest problem areas are likely to be:

- *Dirty power generation*: The world is desperately hungry for energy, with blackouts increasingly common even in the developed world. Some Western governments are making efforts to get this energy from clean sources, such as wind power, but the world's biggest current and future polluters, such as the US, China and India, will remain overwhelmingly reliant on fossil fuel-based power generation, and increasingly on coal, the dirtiest source of power. Technological advances in the future may make coal power a cleaner option, but power plants have 50-year lifespans, so it is the ones built today that will determine pollution levels for the next few decades.

- *Refuse and waste*: Even developed nations are struggling with difficult questions about waste disposal in the future.

In Britain, for instance, which is generally considered to be a good handler of waste, it is estimated that by the early 2020s over 2,000 new waste management sites will be needed in addition to those already present. Local communities, however, almost inevitably bitterly oppose new sites because of the associated health and environmental concerns. So where will the waste go? Generation of hi-tech waste is increasing at an estimated 5 per cent per year (three times faster than 'normal' waste), and this is likely to increase dramatically in the future. Given that these issues pose serious problems for developed countries, how will developing nations fare as their own waste production rates increase to match their developing economies?

- *Vehicle fumes*: There have been major advances in vehicle technology as far as emissions are concerned, so that new vehicles, individually, produce far fewer emissions than in the past. Unfortunately in many areas this has been more than offset by increases in the number of vehicles on the road (doubled in the last two decades), the miles driven and the average size of cars (bigger engines produce more pollution). This means that in Los Angeles, for instance, air quality is now getting worse again after years of improvement.

  In the developing world, the outlook for traffic fumes may be bleaker. Cars there are much more likely to be old, with high emissions, and while the quality of vehicles may improve in the future, the real issue is rocketing levels of traffic. In China, for instance, car ownership increased 130-fold between 1980 and 2001, and although the market there has slowed recently the government has plans to increase domestic car production four-fold by 2010. Vehicle sales in India are also accelerating massively, and very high rates of growth can also be found in Mexico, Brazil and many other developing nations.

Other forms of transport are also set to increase in volume. Shipping is a major source of particulates, nitrogen oxides and sulphur (marine diesel can contain up to 500 times more sulphur than road vehicle diesel). By 2010 it is estimated that cargo ships will account for 75 per cent of European sulphur emissions. As world trade increases, so will marine traffic. Meanwhile air traffic has quadrupled in the last 20 years, and the growth is accelerating as increasing affluence in developing nations boosts demand.

These are just three examples of how pollution is likely to get worse in the future. There are numerous others, from the likelihood of increased agricultural pollution as demand for food puts pressure on farmers to increase yields, to the enhanced threat of nuclear pollution as more nuclear plants are built to make up shortfalls in fossil fuel-based energy production.

Collectively these sources of pollution place a heavy and worsening load on the environment, and we can expect consequences from deteriorating human health to mountains of garbage that swamp our cities; from choking storms of toxic dust to dead zones around our coastlines. Even if these doomsday scenarios are dismissed, the most hardened environmental sceptic cannot dispute that the problems posed by pollution exacerbate the many other threats to the ecosystem covered in this chapter. If nothing else, pollution limits our options for dealing with the other aspects of environmental crisis by degrading our common resources – the air, the soil and the water.

Likelihood: 7
Damage: 5
Fear factor: 6

The hydroxyl holocaust

Hydroxyl radicals are short-lived, highly energetic molecules consisting of a single oxygen atom and a single hydrogen atom. They are created when a water molecule is hit by an energetic particle (usually a photon from sunlight), knocking away one of the hydrogen atoms. The resulting molecule is highly reactive and quickly oxidises another molecule, such as an atmospheric pollutant like sulphur dioxide, in the process getting its other hydrogen molecule back and becoming water again. Usually there is a small, constantly recycling population of hydroxyl radicals in the atmosphere, at the level of about one part per trillion.

Hydroxyl radicals are important in the context of air pollution because they act as molecular scrubbers, helping to keep the atmosphere clean by encouraging the breakdown of pollutants or their conversion into easily soluble forms, so that they can then be dissolved by atmospheric moisture. Without them, pollution would linger for much longer and would stay in the air, with severe impacts on human health. Unfortunately the growing levels of air pollution threaten to soak up hydroxyl radicals faster than they are produced, and some scientists fear that at some point a threshold will be reached where levels of hydroxyl suddenly collapse, and cannot recover without a total absence of pollution. At this point civilisation would experience what has been described as a 'hydroxyl holocaust'.

What will happen if hydroxyl levels collapse?

Air pollution would simply fail to break down and would instead linger as smog. Smog is a soup of toxic gases and particulates that forms when atmospheric conditions prevent the mixing or clearing of air over an area (typically a city in a valley, such as Los Angeles). It is often worsened by the effects of sunlight, which cause the smog chemicals to become highly reactive and therefore much more toxic. Without hydroxyl radicals, however, smog would not be limited to specific areas or days when certain conditions arose. Instead there could be vast clouds of poisonous smog, blanketing cities and whole countries. Millions and possibly billions would be killed directly, while there would also be terrible knock-on effects for agriculture and the natural world that could threaten the basis of civilisation.

Has it happened before?

Mankind has never before been able to influence the make-up of the atmosphere to the extent necessary to trigger a hydroxyl meltdown. It is a measure of the scale of air pollution today that this scenario can even be considered.

How likely is it to happen?

Fears about declining levels of hydroxyl in the atmosphere first surfaced during the 1980s but the picture has been muddied by the complexity of hydroxyl chemistry (in some conditions additional pollution can actually boost hydroxyl levels) and by an apparent resurgence in hydroxyl levels during the 1990s. This may in turn have been the result of the thinning ozone layer, which increased the amount of energetic UV radiation hitting the atmosphere, in which case efforts to let the ozone layer regenerate could once again make hydroxyl levels vulnerable, especially given the accelerating problem of air pollution. In a report in 2001, the UN's Intergovernmental Panel on Climate Change (IPCC, the primary world authority on atmospheric science) took the hydroxyl issue seriously enough to warn of 'the possibility that future emissions might overwhelm the oxidative capacity of the troposphere' (ie the atmosphere's capacity to break down pollution).

Even if this doomsday scenario is unlikely, the IPCC warns that levels of smog chemicals, such as carbon monoxide and nitrogen oxides, can be expected to triple by 2050, while hydroxyl levels may fall by at least 20 per cent by 2100. So even by this estimate lingering smog could be a devastating problem in the future.

Likelihood: 2
Damage: 7
Fear factor: 3

Toxic time bomb

Human activities have caused a vast range of substances to enter the environment, either for the first time ever (because they did not exist until humans started manufacturing them) or at much greater levels than would occur naturally (because of extraction and industrial processing). Even the wildest, most remote areas, apparently free of any marks of human activity, such as the extreme polar regions or the open ocean, bear this imprint of human activity. As a result, humans and animals alike are exposed to a soup of 'unnatural' chemicals: there are around 70,000 chemicals on the market, with new ones appearing at a rate of 1,500 a year. The evidence shows that many of these chemicals persist in the environment, and that they accumulate in greater amounts and at higher concentrations as they pass up through the food chain.

Every new chemical that is released onto the market, and into the environment, adds to the 'body burden' or 'toxic load'. These terms describe the concept that, while individual chemicals may not be present in our bodies at high enough levels to cause detectable problems, cumulatively and collectively they stress the body and damage health. Studies on safety and toxicity generally focus on chemicals in isolation, but we are exposed to a cocktail of chemicals, and very little is known about possible 'cocktail effects'. The anxiety is that with all these unknowns we may be storing up a time bomb for human health, and that at some point the body burden or toxic load may cross a threshold, with catastrophic consequences for health. In particular, there is concern about the effects of this cocktail of persistent and bioaccumulative chemicals on children. Children are much more susceptible to toxic effects, because chemicals have greatest impact during development, and their smaller size increases the effective concentration of the chemicals. The WHO warns that we may 'be conducting a large-scale experiment with children's health'.

What will happen if the toxic time bomb goes off?

Toxic overload could cause a whole range of health effects, but there are three main areas of concern:

- *Persistent organic pollutants (POPS)*: POPs are chemicals that do not get broken down quickly by natural processes or once ingested. They tend to accumulate in the blood, liver and fatty tissues of animals. Among the most notorious are polychlorinated biphenyls (PCBs), which are linked to cancer, suppressed immune function, developmental abnormalities and birth defects, and are thought to have contributed towards declining populations of polar bears, seals, wild salmon and other large animals. PCBs are so dangerous that they are now banned, but high levels persist in the Arctic environment. More worryingly, a new and unregulated class of POPs called brominated flame retardants (BFRs), which have similar effects to PCBs, are turning up in the environment. Dioxins are POPs produced by many industrial processes, and are linked to suppressed immune function, cognitive disorders (mental problems) and endometriosis (a condition in which the lining of the womb appears elsewhere in the body) in both animals and humans. This is just a handful of the POPs that are out there accumulating in the environment and threatening human and animal health.

- *Endocrine disruptors:* Many POPs act as endocrine disruptors: chemicals that mimic the effect of hormones in animals and therefore disrupt their natural hormone levels. Effects include feminisation and infertility, birth and developmental defects, and possibly immune suppression and cancer. Populations of algae, molluscs, fish, frogs and newts in river systems around the world have suffered as a result. A source of endocrine disruptors that particularly affects the human water supply is the contraceptive pill. Women taking the Pill have high levels of oestrogen in their urine, which becomes part of sewage effluent and may not be removed by treatment. Some experts argue that declining sperm counts and rising rates of infertility are linked to this problem.

- *Lead and mercury:* Lead is probably the most significant environmental chemical in terms of human health. At high concentrations it can cause brain damage, and according to scientists in the US even low levels of lead can lower IQ, cause behavioural problems and are strongly correlated with criminality.

  Mercury is a highly toxic metal that is produced by coal-fired power stations and other industry, and is also used in many consumer technology products. It can cause IQ and motor deficiencies. Mercury bioaccumulates to such an extent that pregnant women are advised to limit their consumption of fish in order to avoid ingesting too much.

An age of illness

If environmental levels of POPs, endocrine disruptors and toxic metals such as mercury and lead continue to rise, and to get into people's bodies, existing health infrastructure in the developed world may prove to be woefully inadequate, while the developing world could be altogether overwhelmed. Fertility rates could decline dramatically, while those children that are conceived might have a radically reduced chance of reaching full term. Those that do are much more likely to suffer from malformation or congenital diseases, and as they grow they are likely to be physically and mentally inferior to previous generations. Meanwhile the adult population will see rates of cancer, immune disorders and other degenerative diseases rocket. The natural world will also suffer, with dramatically depleted populations of amphibians and reptiles, which seem to be particularly vulnerable, and the loss of top predators such as polar bears and dolphins.

Has it happened before?

The toxic time bomb threat is worrying precisely because humans have never before been exposed to such a cocktail of artificial chemicals. But there is supposedly one notable historical parallel: the role of lead poisoning in the decline and fall of the Roman Empire. According to this popular theory, lead poisoning was endemic in ancient Rome because of the widespread use of lead in plumbing (in fact the word plumbing derives from the Latin for 'lead': *plumbum*), for serving and cooking dishes, in make-up and as an additive to food and wine for preservative and flavouring purposes. Since the aristocratic classes used the most make-up, drank the most wine, ate the most food and were most likely to enjoy the benefits of expensive preservatives, they suffered most from chronic lead poisoning. Gout, depression and madness became rife, and fertility was seriously impaired. Thus enfeebled, the ruling classes were unable to govern Rome adequately, weakening the state, which was further damaged by less severe, but nonetheless damaging, lead poisoning among the other classes.

There is anecdotal evidence to support some of this theory (eg the apparently high incidence of both insanity and infertility among the emperors of Rome), but it probably shouldn't be taken too seriously. The dangers of lead were well known to the Romans and they may not have consumed quite as much lead as suggested: for instance, the lead pipes of Rome were renowned for being coated with calcium carbonate, which caused plumbing problems but also protected against lead poisoning. More importantly, most experts agree that even if low-level lead poisoning was endemic it probably had little to do with the eventual decline and fall of the Roman Empire, (a more convincing explanation is linked to climate change – see page 153).

How likely is it to happen?

In order to estimate the likelihood of the toxic time bomb going off we need to know two things: is there evidence that dangerous chemicals such as POPs and toxic metals are indeed accumulating in the environment and in people; and can we trust that chemicals that will be released in the future are safe?

Already out there

Disturbingly there is considerable evidence that toxic chemicals are at large. Good places to look for persistent chemicals are the Arctic and the ocean – since there is no industry and practically no people there, we know that any chemicals found in these environments must have come from elsewhere, which means they have lasted for a relatively long time. The evidence is conclusive: there are now far more chemicals turning up in these environments than there used to be. For instance, tests of marine mammals in the 1960s showed the presence of mercury and five organic pollutants; in 2003 over 265 organic pollutants and 50 inorganic chemicals were found in the same species. In the Arctic, high levels of POPs have been recorded in a variety of animals from polar bears to molluscs, while according to the WWF, dioxins have been found at 172 times the acceptable minimum levels for daily intake in whale and dolphin meat in Japanese markets.

There is a similar story for lead and mercury. In the developed world, steps have been taken to limit exposure to lead by phasing it out of petrol and paint, but it is still present at low levels. According to the WHO, up to 30 per cent of urban children show high levels of lead in their blood in some parts of Europe, while globally 15 to 18 million children in developing countries suffer permanent brain damage from lead poisoning. According to an EU commission on mercury, 'Although most people in Europe appear to be within internationally accepted safe levels for exposure, there is evidence that some people are around or above these levels, especially in coastal areas of Mediterranean countries and the Arctic.' In the US, despite drastic cuts in mercury emissions, one in twelve women of childbearing age has blood mercury levels that could hinder brain development in a foetus, according to the Environmental Protection Agency.

Can we trust the chemical companies?

The chemicals industry argues that known toxins, such as mercury, lead and dioxins, have been identified and are now under control or being phased out, and that the regulations regarding new chemicals are so strict that human health is adequately safeguarded. Does this mean that we shouldn't be so concerned? Unfortunately not. Current testing regulations are not as strict as the industry would have us believe. For instance, of the 70,000 chemicals on the market, 30,000 have not been properly tested for their health risks. This is partly because of 'grandfather' laws that make up part of the regulation regime, which say that chemicals that have been in use for a long enough period don't need to meet new standards or undergo testing. Even for those that have, officially, been 'properly' tested, there are many doubts. In general there is no independent testing of chemicals by regulatory bodies – they rely on tests conducted by the manufacturers. This system is clearly open to abuse, and indeed there are numerous incidents of chemical manufacturers twisting regulations, selectively interpreting or suppressing negative results, not making full disclosure and simply lying about their own testing processes.

Given what we know about past failures to spot dangerous chemicals before they were released (eg PCBs), many health and environmental groups argue that regulation of new chemicals should be based on the 'precautionary principle'. This principle is: if there is uncertainty about possible unknown/future effects of a chemical, industry should proceed with caution and not produce the chemical, rather than assuming it is safe to proceed since there is no current evidence of danger. So is the precautionary principle likely to be applied in the future? In a major policy advance the European Union is planning to bring in a new regulation regime that *is* based on the precautionary principle. However, according to Senior WHO official Dr Roberto Bertollini, who is in charge of the special health and environment programme at the WHO's Europe HQ, the industry is resisting fiercely and dishonestly:

> *What I am seeing now is the industry ... producing an extremely biased view of the literature on chemicals and children's health, in a very peculiar way. What the industry is doing is using uncertainty to deny that there are any effects. Yet the industry is denying that there is a link even when it is scientifically established, like the one between particulates and respiratory disease. There's absolutely no doubt there. And the industry is saying this is not true. I have no proof of this, but I think it's trying to exert pressure at EU level ... to soften the regulations.*
>
> *We want a dialogue with the industry, based on a correct interpretation and understanding of the scientific evidence ... We can't have a dialogue when we start from a biased interpretation of the evidence.*

At the very least then, the chemical industry's claims that the public is safeguarded should perhaps be approached with scepticism.

Is the toxic time bomb already going off?

The most alarming evidence that the toxic time bomb *will* threaten human health is that it already *is*. The past few decades have seen alarming rises in the incidences of several major conditions in the developed world – rises that tend to be mirrored in developing nations as they adopt more affluent lifestyles. This has led some commentators to describe the conditions as 'diseases of civilisation'. Examples include childhood asthma, diabetes, cancer, Alzheimer's disease, autism and allergies. This is not to draw a direct or simplistic link between specific forms of pollution and specific conditions; the situation with many of them is complex. For instance, the incidence of asthma has more than doubled in the last two decades in the US, but in Britain decades of increasing incidence have recently levelled off. On balance, however, the evidence is worryingly suggestive. The increasing body burden of toxic chemicals may not end civilisation, but it could seriously lower the quality and length of life for future generations.

Likelihood: 6
Damage: 3
Fear factor: 5

The parched Earth

The world is currently facing a dire water crisis; a crisis that, in the near future, could translate into a full-blown catastrophe. The UN estimates that 40 per cent of the world's population – currently around 2.6 billion people – are without adequate sanitation, and that 1.1 billion people have no access to clean water at all. The health toll is enormous. One child dies every 8 seconds from water-borne diseases, and more than 5 million people a year in total. Even the economic cost is desperate – in Africa alone, over 40 billion work hours are lost each year in the struggle to fetch drinking water. Agriculture is the world's major consumer of water. Globally it accounts for 70 per cent of water consumption, rising to 90 per cent in the developing world. But two fifths of the world's population live in areas suffering water shortages that mean they struggle to get enough water for their crops.

At the heart of the current crisis is the rocketing demand for water, demand that is set to increase still further in the future. Between 1900 and 1995 water consumption increased at double the rate of population growth, and this is set to accelerate as developing nations struggle to reach developed world standards of living, with concomitant levels of water consumption.

What will happen if the water runs out?

The situation for many parts of the world is already grim, but if the water crisis is not solved things will get much worse. By 2015 the UN estimates that 2.4 billion people will have no access to clean water, and by 2025 two thirds of the world's population will be living in water-stressed countries. Agriculture will suffer accordingly, especially in the most vulnerable areas. In Africa, for instance, according to the Consultative Group on International Agricultural Research, annual crop loss by 2025 could equal the entire crop production of the US and India put together, and the region will face a 23 per cent shortfall. In China, water shortages mean the country could be dependent on imported grain within a few years. The end result will be escalating rates of water-borne disease, caused by lack of sanitation and the need to use sewage as fertiliser, together with famine on a massive scale as agriculture fails in the poorest parts of the world.

Water wars

Competition for water is already a source of tension in many parts of the world. If supply fails to keep up with demand, tension could lead to conflict. In the Middle East, for instance, Syria and Iraq are at loggerheads with Turkey over management of the Tigris-Euphrates system, while in the Near East there are arguments between Israel, Jordan and the Palestinians over the River Jordan and underground aquifers. In East Africa, Ethiopian suggestions about renegotiating the distribution of water from the Nile have already drawn warnings from Egypt that it will use force if necessary.

The Nile is probably the world's major potential flashpoint for water conflict, given that Egypt is already planning to increase the amount of Nile water it uses for irrigation in order to feed its rapidly growing population, while other East African countries want to do likewise. According to former UN Secretary General Dr Boutros Boutros Ghali, failure to make some sort of treaty will 'certainly [lead to] military confrontation between countries in the region ... The next war among countries will not be for oil or territorial borders, but only for the problem of water.'

Has it happened before?

Water scarcity has played a role in the collapse of many past societies, usually in conjunction with related issues such as habitat destruction or loss of soil fertility. The civilisations of Mesopotamia (c.4000–1200 BCE), also known as the Fertile Crescent, tended to rise and fall according to their water resources, which in turn depended on climate change in the region. Mesopotamia was made up of city-states, each of which supported a large population through central control of irrigation and food distribution networks. When water scarcity caused crops to fail for several years in succession, the population of a city-state would gradually concentrate in the central city, abandoning the more vulnerable outlying villages, until the food ran out entirely. Social order would break down, leading to rioting and fighting, followed by mass migration or simple starvation. Similar scenes were repeated in societies such as the Mayans of Central America, where densely populated empires crumbled in the face of drought (c. 800 CE), and the ancient Indus Valley Culture, whose major cities such as Harappa and Mohenjo Daro declined around 1750 BCE when a major river changed course and eventually dried up.

On the whole, however, societies have become much less vulnerable to water shortages as transport and communications have improved. Water can now be shipped around directly, or food can be transported instead, to make up for crop failures caused by local water shortages. In the near future, however, water scarcity could become a global phenomenon, so that only by making real sacrifices will the few water-rich parts of the world be able to supply the water-poor parts with enough to meet their needs.

How likely is it to happen?

The most telling evidence that a water crisis is incipient comes from the current plight of the world's main sources of water – aquifers (underground water flows) and rivers and lakes.

Aquifers provide a vital lifeline for communities in dry areas, but they are easily over-exploited by their very nature. Often aquifers are the result of thousands or millions of years of slow accumulation of water. If left untapped they can build up into a substantial reserve, but since the rate of replenishment is so low, what seems at first like an inexhaustible reserve can quickly become irreversibly depleted.

This is exactly what is happening at numerous places around the world. In China, for instance, some 30 cubic kilometres of water are being taken out of the ground each year. Mexico City is sucking water out of its underground aquifers so fast that the entire city has sunk 9 metres in the last century, while a million of its residents are dependent on water trucks. In the US, the Ogallala aquifer that supplies a third of the country's irrigation water could run out within 60 years according to some estimates.

In India the situation is even worse. The widespread availability of cheap pumps and the inadequacy of the official water supply system means that millions of farmers have sunk unregulated bore holes to extract water from aquifers, sucking 200 cubic kilometres out of the ground each year. In Gujarat, for instance, the water table is dropping by 6 metres a year. As the larger, richer farms sink boreholes up to a kilometre deep, half of India's traditional wells have been left high and dry (up to 95 per cent in some areas), leading to an epidemic of suicides amongst small farmers. A million new holes are bored each year, and the power demands of the pumps lead to widespread blackouts. Soon, experts predict, the entire system will collapse, leading to anarchy in rural India. This pattern is being repeated across Asia as small pumps and deep boreholes catch on from Pakistan to Vietnam, and water tables plunge accordingly.

Rivers and lakes across the globe are also suffering, mainly due to water extraction for thirsty agricultural programmes. China's Yellow River now runs dry for 200 plus days of the year (compared to just 10 in 1988) and Lake Chad in Africa has shrunk by 95 per cent since 1960. The Aral Sea in Central Asia was once the world's fourth largest inland sea, but has shrunk to a tiny fragment of its former self, mainly thanks to rivers being diverted to feed cotton fields. What's left is an arid wasteland of salt flats, polluted with toxic heavy metals that cause some of the highest cancer and infant mortality rates in the world; an apocalyptic vision of a world that has failed to meet its water management challenges.

Even highly developed nations are affected. The major river systems of Australia are in crisis thanks to decades of mismanagement, yet many of the most populous areas of Australia depend on them for water. The result is that, according to Australian water expert Professor Peter Cullen, 'Some of our major [cities] are really in a race at the moment to see who's going to run out of water first.'

Can the water crisis be resolved?

Currently the main responses to the water crisis have been to increase the role of the private sector and to invest in megaprojects such as dams and water-redistribution canals. The private sector can help to overcome some of the physical issues in water management, such as leaky infrastructure that wastes water (in Mexico City, for instance, 27 per cent of the water supply is lost through leaks in pipes), or wasteful consumption of water (too often considered a 'free' resource). In practice, however, private sector involvement has mostly worked out badly, especially in the developing world. High prices and poor regulation lead to resentment and protest, with the result that many of the multinationals have pulled out of risky areas leaving the market to less competent and scrupulous players. Also, private sector involvement cannot solve water problems that have political or social roots. Finally, there is a moral argument that water resources should be a common resource, and that it is wrong to privatise them.

Mega-projects also have a mixed record. Projects of one sort or another affect 60 per cent of the world's large rivers but have often caused more harm than good, displacing populations, destroying ecosystems, and failing due to siltation. Examples include China's Three Gorges Dam, which has faced massive opposition from environmental groups as well as causing much social injustice; or Australia's diversion of the Snowy River, which has had to be partially restored in a belated attempt to undo ecological damage.

Many commentators call for more money and effort to be spent on natural or low-tech solutions. Restoring wetlands, for instance, would help to regulate water flow and conserve water sources, while simple methods like encouraging drip irrigation over spraying can make a big difference. The potential impact of such solutions offers cause for optimism, but the major decision makers may not be paying attention. At the World Water Forum in 2002, the World Bank, the International Monetary Fund, the UN and others met with politicians from hundreds of countries, but the focus of the meeting was very much on mega-projects.

Water optimists argue that the crisis will be resolved through market forces or technology. For instance, some argue that trade in 'virtual water' will even out inequalities in supply. Virtual water is the water contained in crops and other goods that are shipped from water-rich countries to water-poor ones. Growing wheat, for instance, in water-rich parts of South America and transporting it to water-poor Australia, would effectively make up the latter's water deficit (ironically, Australia is at present a net exporter of water thanks to beef exports). But virtual water transfer relies on trade and mass transport, which cost money and energy, both in short or diminishing supply, especially in the poorest, most vulnerable water-stressed areas. Other experts point to increased use of desalinisation as a way to make up water shortfalls, but this is also energy-costly and causes environmental headaches by creating brine mountains.

A dry future

The bottom line is that there should be enough water on the planet to meet everyone's needs, but to accomplish this the developed world will have to rethink its water consumption and make changes to its way of life. More seriously, millions of people in the developing world face the prospect of worsening water crises leading to poverty, disease and famine and increasing the potential for mass migration and conflict. The greatest potential for catastrophe, however, comes from the likely impact on habitats such as wetlands and forests, with knock-on effects for biodiversity, and from the threat to agriculture. India's massive population growth, set to make it the world's most populous nation by 2030, has been sustained through a massive expansion in its agriculture, but the whole basis of this agricultural revolution is now threatened by aquifer and river depletion. The same applies throughout much of Asia and elsewhere in the world. It is hard to see how the world's poorest countries will afford to pay for vast quantities of food grown in distant parts of the world, assuming this food is available at all.

Likelihood: 7
Damage: 4
Fear factor: 6

The barren land

If you were asked to picture a farmer on his land, you would probably call to mind an image of someone crumbling moist, dense, black soil between his fingers, as vigorous green shoots burst forth from the good earth all around him. But what if that soil was a dry, dusty covering, blown aside by the slightest gust to reveal salt, sand and hard stones? How could anything grow in such a barren land?

This scenario is fast becoming a reality for large parts of the Earth's arable land, from far-flung desert countries to the breadbaskets of Europe and America. So while growing population and increasing affluence mean that global food demand is predicted to rise by 60 per cent, the area of quality land available on which to grow food is actually shrinking alarmingly. A number of factors seriously threaten to strip the Earth's arable land of its fertile topsoil and reduce it to a sterile salty wasteland of sand and dust that barely covers the ugly bedrock beneath. These factors include soil erosion, salinisation, soil fertility loss and competition for land use.

- *Erosion*: Soil is eroded from cultivated land at between 500 and 10,000 times the rate it is eroded from forested land, and between 10 and 40 times faster than it is replaced by natural processes. The main culprits behind soil erosion are deforestation and land clearance, poor farming techniques (eg overgrazing), droughts, and poor water management.

- *Salinisation*: Salinisation is an increase in the salt content of soil, which can have a direct toxic effect on plants, and also makes it harder for them to absorb water from the soil. Salt is also highly corrosive to buildings and infrastructure, and threatens human health. Salinisation can be caused by mobilisation of salt already in the ground (usually as a result of land clearance and use of land for agriculture), or by build up of salt from irrigation water. Once it has occurred it is incredibly hard to get rid of; even with a steady supply of fresh irrigation water, it can take up to 500 years to flush salt out of the soil.

- *Soil fertility loss*: Even in areas that appear to have a healthy layer of topsoil, the soil has often taken a battering in terms of fertility and nutrient levels. Simply opening up land for agriculture exposes the richest topsoil to erosion, while in many parts of the world, especially in tropical areas, the majority of nutrients in an ecosystem are present in the natural land cover, rather than the soil itself. Clearing the land thus strips out most of the nutrients, while the first one or two crops grown on the land extract what is left. Even in areas where soil fertility is high, the delicate systems that build and maintain that fertility can be damaged or shattered by intensive agriculture – especially by the use of fertilisers and pesticides, which tend to kill off important fertility-maintaining organisms such as earthworms. Other processes such as soil acidification or alkalinisation, caused by industrial pollution and damaging farming techniques, also degrade soil quality.

- *Competition for land use*: Agriculture is not the only use for land. The main competition for land comes from urban and transport development, which can lead to land being paved or concreted over.

What will happen if the land is ruined?

Accelerated erosion of arable soils could cause an enormous loss of soil on a global scale – as much as 1,000 tonnes a second, or 20–30 billion tonnes a year. Soil that is lost to erosion is typically the best soil, between 1.3 and 5 times richer in organic matter than the soil that remains. Eroded soils also lose their ability to absorb water, so that more rainfall is lost to evaporation and runoff. The eroded material also blocks up rivers and chokes coral reefs and other marine habitats, as well as posing a threat to human respiratory health.

If soil erosion goes too far it leads to desertification, where formerly arable land becomes arid or semi-arid and starts to resemble a desert. According to alarmist estimates, as much as a third of the Earth's surface is currently threatened by desertification. But the picture is complicated by the relationship between desertification and changes in climate and distribution of rainfall. For instance, in Africa, higher rainfall in recent years (after the droughts of the 1970s and 80s) has led to a full-scale retreat of the sands of the Sahara, and a widespread 'greening' of the Sahel, the sub-Saharan arid zone. However, this recent retreat comes after long years of steady expansion, probably linked to rainfall changes caused by air pollution and global dimming – testament to the possible impact of a similar phenomenon in densely populated South and East Asia.

In the developed world vast areas of land have been paved over to make way for roads and car parks – often the flat, well-drained land most suitable for agriculture. If this trend continues, some of the world's best farmland could be lost, and natural habitats will come under threat.

Soils that survive erosion or being paved over could nevertheless become useless for farming. Degraded soil quality also has a direct effect on human health, because it reduces the levels of nutrients in food grown on the soil. Many health experts today argue that low-level mineral deficiencies in the population are epidemic as a result, and are major contributors to rising rates of chronic/degenerative diseases.

The combined effect of these threats to the soil could lead to a massive global loss of arable land. Estimates of the proportion of the world's arable land that is already severely damaged range from 20 to 80 per cent, and soil degradation has actually reduced global agricultural productivity by 13 per cent since the 1950s. Estimates for the future are alarming: by 2025 about a fifth of arable land in South America is expected to degrade or disappear, as is a third of the arable land in Asia and an astonishing two-thirds of the arable land in Africa.

Marginal land

As the availability of high quality land decreases and demand for food production increases, one inevitable result is an increase in the cultivation of marginal land – land that is not really suitable for agriculture because of aridity, fragile fertility, vulnerability to erosion, distance from population and other reasons. Bringing this land under cultivation further threatens both the environment and the long-term security of food supplies. People who depend on food grown on marginal land are much more vulnerable to environmental changes such as climate change, droughts and ecological breakdown.

Has it happened before?

Soil loss and degradation that forces the exploitation of marginal land has led to disaster for many societies in history, including the Anasazi Indians of North America, the Mayans of Central America, and the Polynesians of Easter Island, to name just a few.

The Anasazi were the society that built the grand pueblos that can still be seen in the US Southwest. Broadly speaking, they flourished from 600 to 1400 CE, but their society collapsed soon after they began farming marginal lands to feed their burgeoning population. Drought conditions that they had previously been able to weather were exacerbated by environmental damage they had caused. This led to failure of agriculture on the marginal land, which in turn meant they could no longer feed themselves. The result was catastrophic social breakdown with conflict and enforced migration.

A classic example of the dangers of salinisation can be found in the Middle East, where much of the area historically known as the Fertile Crescent is now sterile. Salinisation was a major contributor to the collapse of this area as a centre of ancient civilisation.

How likely is to happen?

The facts and figures about the soil loss and degradation that has already happened make grim reading. Rampant soil erosion has already stripped much of the world's arable land of valuable topsoil: Iowa, one of the most agriculturally productive states in the US, has lost about half of its topsoil over the last century; in China, 19 per cent of the land surface is affected by soil erosion, which dumps some 5 billion tonnes of soil into rivers and the sea each year.

Over the last twenty years desertification has claimed land equivalent to all the farmland in the US. The UN Environment Programme has warned that 45 per cent of Africa is in the grip of desertification, while over 25 per cent of China has been affected.

Salinisation already affects land all over the world, blighting millions of acres of the Great Plains and California's Central Valley in the US, as well as 9 per cent of land in China and 9 per cent of arable land in Australia, including much of what was previously the most productive farmland. It is predicted that a third of Australia's wheat belt will be lost to salinisation over the next 20 years, and up to 25 per cent of its arable land in total. Soil fertility loss has decreased by half the amount of farmland in China that can be classed as high quality. Competition for land use has seen around 16 million hectares (61,000 square miles) of the US paved over for transport and urban development.

In other words, enormous damage has already been done, by processes that are generally continuing or accelerating. For instance, poor water management and land clearance are the major factors behind erosion and desertification, and they are almost guaranteed to get worse over the next few decades, while a combination of short-term profit-taking and a lack of both knowledge and training hampers efforts to improve farming techniques that might preserve the soil.

Competition for land use is also hotting up as car owner-ship in the developing world and accompanying urban and road development accelerate. In Europe and Japan, an average of 0.02 hectare is paved over for every vehicle. If China were to achieve similar levels of car ownership and pave over land accordingly, it would lose 13 million hectares of land – equivalent to more than half of its rice-growing arable land. Rapid urbanisation and development in other parts of the developing world similarly threaten to eat into available land.

Can we save the soil?

There are many tried and tested techniques that could help to safeguard the world's soils – some of them date back to ancient times: reforestation holds soils together; integrated farming techniques combine crops to allow harvesting without exposing the soil or stripping its fertility; organic farming reduces levels of fertilisers and pesticides; and drip irrigation conserves water and prevents salinisation. However, the chances of these relatively simple techniques being adopted on a global basis look slim. In reality, the situation is likely to worsen as pressure to produce more food combines with poor farming techniques to put more unsuitable land under poorly managed irrigation. In any case, a huge amount of effectively irreversible damage has already been done. To fully understand the potential impact of the soil crisis, however, you need to see it in the context of the wider global food crisis.

Likelihood: 7
Damage: 5
Fear factor: 6

The coming famine

In an age of plenty, few in the Western world can remember what it feels like to go hungry, or imagine what it must be like not to know whether you'll be able to find enough to eat next week. Could this really happen to us? Empty supermarkets and closed restaurants, hungry crowds squabbling over food aid packages and long queues for soup kitchens?

During the 1960s, the doomsday prophecies *du jour* were warnings of famine along classic Malthusian lines: that population growth would outstrip food production; that there would be mass famines when there were too many people to feed. Fortunately these prophecies have not been fulfilled, because although world population has doubled since 1960, food production has not only managed to keep up, but has allowed more people to eat more and higher quality food than ever before. World grain consumption has more than doubled since 1970, and meat consumption has tripled since 1961.

But this doesn't mean that the world has avoided a food crisis. Worldwide, the proportion of the population who are malnourished decreased from 37 per cent to 18 per cent from the mid-1960s to the mid-90s, but the massive growth in total population means that vast and growing numbers of people remain malnourished. Currently malnutrition is the underlying cause of half of all child deaths, and causes 10 million deaths a year in total. In 2003, according to the UN Food and Agriculture Organisation, 840 million people were malnourished or lacked food security (the certainty that they will be able to get enough to eat).

Worse still, the predicted growth in demand for food is alarming. The number of people who are malnourished or lack food security is projected to increase by a staggering

2 billion people by 2025, with 60 per cent more food needed over the next 30 years to feed the Earth's swelling population. It seems that the warnings about famine and disaster may have been prematurely dismissed, and that the Green Revolution of the last four decades has simply given us a stay of execution, deferring the nightmare scenario but not defeating it.

What will happen if the world runs out of food?

In the developed world, the most likely scenario is that we will not be able to go on expecting to eat more but pay less. At present, the price of the food we buy does not reflect the true cost of agriculture in a global sense – eg the cost in water resources, damage to land and social injustice. This may be why a recent report reveals that in Britain an amazing 33 per cent of food is simply thrown in the bin. This kind of profligacy will almost certainly become a thing of the past, as food in the developed world becomes much more expensive. We will probably be forced to change our consumption patterns, eating less meat and much less fish, and relying more on locally grown and seasonally available cheaper foodstuffs. Ironically, this is exactly what environmental groups advocate at present.

In the developing world the picture could be much grimmer. So much of the population there already exists on the margins of food security. Any one of the problem areas outlined above, such as water scarcity or soil erosion, could push them over the edge. On balance, it does not seem unlikely that this will happen, leading to large-scale famine in particularly vulnerable parts of the world such as India or

Pakistan, and chronic food insecurity in much of the rest of the world.

Has it happened before?

A historical parallel for the looming food crisis might be the Irish Potato Famine of the 1840s. Actually the culmination of a number of famines, the Great Hunger, triggered by a wave of potato blight but exacerbated by poor weather and astonishing official indifference, led to mass starvation on the very doorstep of 'civilised' Europe. More than 1.5 million people died (nearly 20 per cent of the population) and a further million emigrated. While the millions died, food was still being *exported* from Ireland to Britain. The tragedy could have been avoided before it happened and alleviated while it was going on, but for the dictates of free market economics and the characteristics of the social and agricultural system of the time.

How likely is it to happen?

The twin forces driving us towards a food crisis are growing demand on the one hand, and the threat that agriculture will not be able to sustain even current levels of supply, on the other.

The threat to agriculture

Many of the other issues dealt with in this chapter and the next are major threats to agriculture. Probably the most serious of these are the looming water crisis (which is predicted to hit agriculture hardest because agriculture is the world's major user of water) and the threat to the world's soils. Meanwhile pollution degrades land and reduces the area available for agriculture, and can also damage crops directly.

Climate change is a great unknown, but it is feared that it may lead to catastrophic shifts in rainfall patterns – such as causing failure of the monsoon, which could threaten the agriculture of South and East Asia, where most of the world's population live. On the other hand, it may increase yields in many parts of the world. However, hopes that any negative effects will be counterbalanced by opening up previously unproductive regions to agriculture, such as the Siberian and Canadian tundra, are ill-founded. Because of their latitude these regions receive less sunlight than more tropical regions, and their soils may not be suitable for intensive agriculture.

Pesticide resistance is a growing problem, brought on by massive and inefficient use of pesticides. As far back as 1996, there were over 500 species of pesticide-resistant insects and mites, along with 270 weed species, 150 plant diseases and 6 species of rat! Many species now have multiple resistance. The nature of industrial agriculture, with its vast monocultures increasingly made up of genetically identical clones, means that the vulnerability of crops to pests and disease is also set to increase. Dealing with this problem requires more and more potent pesticides, with knock-on effects for wildlife. Human ingenuity is probably up to the challenge of pesticide resistance, especially since there is a strong profit motive for biotech and chemical companies, but it could well be another severe limiter on efforts to increase agricultural production.

Introduced organisms, also known as 'alien' organisms (because they are not indigenous), are a huge and growing problem. They include plants, animals and diseases. Highly invasive weeds, for instance, now cover vast tracts of farmland and waterways in many parts of the world. As well as crowding out productive plants and upsetting local ecosystems, they may also be toxic to livestock and contribute to soil erosion. In his book *Collapse: How Societies Choose to Fail or Survive*, Jared Diamond describes how invasive weeds have ruined up to 90 per cent of grazing in the US state of Montana at a cost of $100 million a year, while in Australia some 3,000 weed species do more than $3 billion of damage a year.

Animals can also compete with livestock for food – the classic example being the introduction of rabbits into Australia, which reduced by half the amount of available pasture for sheep and cattle, as well as contributing to land degradation.

The photosynthetic limit

Sunlight is commonly touted as an inexhaustible resource, and it is true that man does not harness the vast majority of the energy that hits the Earth. In terms of plant growth, however, only a fraction of this energy is available because most of it does not fall on land where plants can grow. The maximum potential plant growth for any area of land is also limited by factors such as latitude (which affects the strength of sunlight), temperature, rainfall, altitude, etc, and by the biology of photosynthesis itself. Adding all these up gives a figure for the photosynthetic limit of the planet – the maximum possible plant growth that could be achieved given the available sunlight.

In 1986 it was estimated that, between agricultural and leisure uses and paved-over land, humans were already 'soaking up' about half of the available photosynthetic capacity. Unless there is a radical change in human activities, population and economic growth mean that mankind will hit the photosynthetic limit by 2050. At this point all the available sunlight that falls on land will be either utilised or wasted by human land uses, with practically none left for natural habitats. Incredibly, then, sunlight may turn out to be the limiting factor that puts a ceiling on human food production and prevents mankind from meeting the needs of the global population.

The meat menace

One of the simplest ways to produce more food with the resources available, and in particular to get around possible water shortages, would be to grow more crops and less meat. Producing protein through livestock or fish farming (see below) is tremendously inefficient. To produce a kilogram of beef takes at least 15 cubic metres of water, while a kilogram of cereals needs 3 cubic metres at most. Livestock also need to be fed, with 34 per cent of world grain production already used as feed. Housing and feeding livestock is adding to land pressure, and natural habitats are losing out (eg South America has seen extensive forest clearance to make way for ranches and soybean plantations for feed). Livestock produce huge quantities of slurry, a pollutant, and even greater amounts of methane, a potent greenhouse gas.

Unfortunately the global appetite for meat is growing at a tremendous rate. Meat consumption has tripled since 1961 and demand is increasing exponentially with increasing affluence in the developing world. Speaking to the BBC, Anders Berntell, executive director of the Stockholm International

Water Institute, an organisation that monitors world water use, warned:

> *it's going to be almost impossible to feed future generations the kind of diet we have now in western Europe and North America ... [increasing demand for meat means] the world's future water supply is a problem that's an entire order of magnitude greater than we've begun to realise.*

Problems with aquaculture

The land is not the only place that food can be grown, and some food commentators point to aquaculture – the farming of fish, prawns, shrimp, etc – as a way to alleviate future food insecurity and secure some of the productive potential of the oceans. Aquaculture is already a major global industry and is growing fast. It has doubled in scale in just fifteen years and already contributes 10 per cent of global aquatic production, with over a 1,000 species either already being cultured or under investigation as culture species. Predictions show that by the year 2035, farmers may produce as many kilograms of fish as they do chicken, while to meet the global demand for fish in the future, aquaculture must grow by 235 to 573 per cent in the next 35 years.

But far from being a shining hope for the future, aquaculture could well turn out to be another nail in the ecological coffin. The environmental impact of aquaculture is enormous. The fish, prawns, etc are reared intensively, in similar conditions to terrestrial livestock, with similar problems. They produce large amounts of waste, which usually go directly into the water supply or the ocean. Aquaculture effluent is a major source of eutrophic blooms, red tides and dead zones. Creating pens and ponds often means damaging natural habitats, especially in tropical areas where vast tracts of vital coastal mangrove forest and swamp have been destroyed. Farmed species are genetically different – and inferior – to wild species, but often escape and contaminate the wild gene pool. Cultured salmon, for instance, have a survival rate 50 times worse than wild salmon. Farmed species have radically higher rates of disease and parasitic infection, and recent research shows that they pass these on to wild fish. Wild salmon tested near a salmon farm in Canada showed parasite infection rates 73 times higher than normal. To combat disease and parasites, farmed fish are treated with high levels of antibiotics and pesticides, which pollute the environment, encourage pest resistance and damage other species.

In the developing world, aquaculture also has a social cost. It is often a major export industry, generating profits for a few exporters without benefiting local people, who are sometimes violently driven off land so that it can be converted to aquaculture. In Bangladesh, for instance, armed gangs breach sea dikes so that salt water will flood rice paddies and ruin local peasants, whereupon the paddies can be bought up for next to nothing.

The fundamental flaw with aquaculture, however, is not the direct environmental or social cost. Much of the fish farmed around the world is carnivorous, and must therefore be fed on protein, making it a ruinously inefficient form of agriculture in ecological terms. The majority of feed at present comes from wild-caught fish, and it takes 20 kilograms of wild fish meat to produce 1 kilogram of farmed fish. Even if wild fishmeal is replaced with soybeans or other crops, aquaculture still poses the same problems as terrestrial meat production.

This is not to say that all aquaculture is ecologically harmful. Cultivation of herbivorous species, raised in existing habitats such as rice paddies where they eat material that would otherwise be waste, can be a valuable contributor to diets in some of the world's most deprived areas. But on a global scale, it seems that aquaculture cannot be a viable route to future food security.

Can the food crisis be solved?

In the post-war years a Green Revolution transformed world agriculture and enabled it to keep pace with and outstrip world population growth. The key elements were fertilisers, pesticides, new varieties and hybrids, mechanisation, irrigation and new farming practices. Many commentators now predict a Second Green Revolution, with GM crops, more mechanisation, and hi-tech systems for ultra-efficient irrigation and fertiliser and pesticide application. There are numerous objections to most of these, however, from the dubious benefits of GM crops to the difficulty of getting hi-tech solutions to the vast majority of the world's farmers, who will simply be too poor to afford the capital investment needed. In fact this scenario could be described as the 'Corporate Agriculture' future.

Even if these objections could be overcome, however, optimism about the potential for a Second Green Revolution may be misplaced. As described above, less and less land is available for agriculture, while other resources such as water and even sunlight may already be close to their limits. In other words there simply may not be a solid enough platform from which a Second Revolution can be launched.

Lean years ahead?

On balance the future for global food security looks bleak. The global situation in the near future could be said to be similar to that of Ireland at the time of the Potato Famine, with the dictates of the globalised market forcing developing nations to export food while millions starve at home, and a developed world where citizens wring their hands but are unwilling to compromise our own lifestyle. Will we find ourselves looking on, and eating food imported from the affected regions, while 20 per cent of the developed world starves and another 12 per cent attempts to emigrate?

Likelihood: 7
Damage: 6
Fear factor: 7

The starving ocean

When the first European fishermen reached the fishing grounds of the Grand Banks, off the coast of North America, they were astonished at the bounty that surrounded them. One only had to dip a basket over the side to bring in a handsome catch of huge, meaty fish. The sea was so thick with life you could almost walk on the water. Surely this marine cornucopia could never be exhausted? Four hundred and fifty years later those fishermen would be gazing down into a marine desert, where the few stunted survivors of a once mighty race nose about in the thin mud of the ocean bottom for scraps of carrion. Today, according to a growing chorus of scientists, the Grand Banks offers a horrible vision of the fate that could lie in store for all the world's oceans, for there is growing alarm that they are being overexploited to the point where all major fisheries will collapse, with knock-on consequences for the global ecosystem.

The annual global catch increased six-fold between 1950 and 1997, with the result that almost all of the industrially fished populations have been reduced to 15–20 per cent of their former levels. Peak catches in both the Pacific and Atlantic oceans were achieved in 1989, and have decreased since. In 2001 in the Northeast Atlantic, for instance, only 16 per cent of fish stocks were within safe biological limits, according to the International Council for the Exploration of the Seas. Most of the rest of the world's fisheries are also under pressure or have already collapsed, most famously the Grand Banks cod fishery off the northeast coast of the US, which was closed in 1992 after experiencing a 99 per cent decline and still has not recovered.

As domestic fisheries decline and collapse, the industrial fishing fleets of the developed world move on to strip the waters of the developing world. The EU, for instance, is currently under fire for buying up fishing licences from corrupt West African governments so that its heavily subsidised fleets can drain fisheries there to the extent that the indigenous fleet sits idle in port, while the seafood-reliant populations are increasingly forced to strip the land of terrestrial wild foods by hunting bush meat in an unsustainable fashion.

The main causes of overfishing are poor fisheries management and the destructive methods used in fishing. For instance, industrial fishing methods now include vast nets with mouths the size of 50 football pitches, or bottom-trawling nets that plough 6 metre-wide furrows in the ocean bottom for kilometres, destroying the entire fragile sea-floor ecosystem. Between a quarter and two thirds of catches are considered 'by-catch' – species accidentally trapped in the same nets as target fish –most of which simply dies and is thrown away. Coral reefs are fished with explosives or poison, which brings short-term increases in yields but destroys the resource in the long-term.

As the major fished species become scarcer, the industry turns to increasingly marginal species. In the Southern Ocean, for instance, krill is becoming a common target. Krill are tiny shrimp-like creatures that would previously have been considered far too small and unappetising for exploitation, but the industry is becoming desperate for protein in any form. Effectively it has been reduced to dredging plankton out of the ocean to compress into generic 'seafood' products.

What will happen if we strip the oceans bare?

About 2 billion people rely on the ocean for most or all of the protein in their diet, so continued industrial fishing threatens their food security. With little or no marine protein available, the developed world would fall back on terrestrial protein sources, but the developing world may not have this luxury, exacerbating the incipient food crisis (see 'The coming famine', above).

With time, fisheries might be expected to recover, except that over-exploitation threatens to permanently alter the genetic make-up of many of the world's most valuable fish species, because of the selection pressure exerted by industrial fishing. Since smaller/younger fish can slip through gaps in nets, heavy fishing has selectively removed those fish with genes for large size and rapid maturation, and left behind those with genes for small size and slow maturation. Recent studies show that these changes, which took only a few decades to cause, could take centuries to reverse, drastically reducing the chances of recovery for collapsed fisheries.

Ocean doomsday

A particularly bleak outlook for the oceans is proposed by writer Debbie MacKenzie, on her website *The Starving Ocean*. She looked at evidence that the Grand Banks cod fishery was not only failing to recover, but was actually becoming more impoverished despite the ban on cod fishing (other fishing continues), and from there developed an ocean doomsday scenario. In a nutshell, her theory is that overfishing has reduced the total biomass of the ocean, which has in turn reduced overall ocean productivity. She posits that a healthy marine ecosystem depends on massive recycling of nitrogen from deep to shallow water, which is accomplished by the migration of vast quantities of zooplankton (tiny animals), the bulk of which consists of fish spawn. With far fewer fish in the ocean, there is much less zooplankton. When algae, fish, etc die and sink to the bottom of the ocean, they take their nutritious nitrogen with them, and with no zooplankton to recycle it to shallow water, the whole ocean food chain breaks down, leading to reduced productivity across the whole system. From whales and cod to barnacles and seaweed, the plants and animals in the ocean effectively starve, and MacKenzie says there is evidence to show that this is exactly what is happening.

Has it happened before?

Some historical societies have suffered greatly from the collapse of fish stocks. The ancient Native American societies of California's Channel Islands suffered food shortages leading to disorder and war, when climate change affected ocean currents that in turn affected local fish stocks. Overfishing by Easter Islanders, leading to collapse of easily fished local stocks, reduced their dietary options when ecological disaster led to crop shortages, and proved to be another nail in their coffin.

Improved seafaring technology has meant that more modern societies have largely been able to overcome problems with local fisheries by simply sending their fishing fleets further afield, but local communities can still be devastated. For example, the communities of Newfoundland that once depended on the Grand Banks fishery for their prosperity are now case studies in social and economic decline. Similar consequences may be felt far beyond the local level, however, because fishing is another example, alongside pollution, for instance, of how human activities are now operating at a scale unmatched in history, and therefore impacting the environment on a scale never seen before. In the future, there may be no new fisheries to exploit and nowhere left for the fishing fleets to go.

How likely is it to happen?

Sustainable fishing should be possible. Experience shows that marine reserves can protect stocks and even help them to recover from over-fishing, and the UK's Royal Commission on Environmental Pollution estimates that to designate and run reserves covering 30 per cent of the world's oceans would cost less than £7.5 billion (roughly $13 billion) a year, less than half the amount currently spent on subsidies for commercial fishing concerns. Currently, however, less than 0.5 per cent of the world's oceans are constituted as reserves, while most of the rest of the oceans are simply open to exploitation with no effective means of regulation or protection.

The establishment, in 1997, of the Marine Stewardship Council (MSC) by the WWF and major industrial partners to certify properly managed fisheries as 'sustainable', offers some grounds for optimism. Progress has been slow, however, with relatively few fisheries passing the certification criteria, and some dispute over the robustness of the verification process. In the long run, however, the success of MSC certification will depend on consumers buying responsibly and being willing to pay higher prices (and not just in the developed world, but in developing markets like China as well). If this model works, the world's remaining fish stocks might be managed successfully, while reserve areas would allow depleted stocks to recover, so that fish can continue to make up a large portion of the global diet.

Unless the MSC model works soon, however, the pessimistic scenario will come to pass, wherein all of the world's major fisheries collapse and the world turns to increasingly marginal marine species, which collapse in turn. By this time the developed world has been reduced to eating non-specific 'marine protein' while the developing world gets no seafood of any kind.

What about the ultra-doomsday scenario proposed by Debbie Mackenzie? Is this a genuine possibility? Given the increasing variety and quantity of biomass being hauled out of the ocean, it is not implausible that human activity could make this kind of dent in the marine ecosystem, while research on ocean acidification and warming seems to back up MacKenzie's thesis (see 'Acid seas', below). What she is effectively describing is a global tipping point, where massive exploitation finally crosses a threshold, with catastrophic results. If she is right the whole ocean ecosystem could be in danger, with terrible consequences for the wider global ecosystem, not to mention the global diet.

Likelihood: 7
Damage: 4
Fear factor: 6

Acid seas

The ocean was the cradle for early life, and still houses the majority of the world's organisms. But what if the ocean were to be transformed into an inhospitable acid bath? This, at least from the point of view of many marine organisms, is the threat posed by rising levels of CO_2 in the atmosphere, which could have disastrous knock-on consequences for the oceans through the twin mechanisms of global warming and ocean acidification.

Much of the carbon dioxide in the atmosphere is dissolved by seawater (20–25 million tonnes a day, according to the Intergovernmental Oceanographic Commission), but this makes the seawater more acidic as it reacts to form carbonic acid. The pH of the oceans has already changed from 8.2 in pre-industrial times to 8.1 today. This may not sound like much, but pH is a logarithmic scale (which means that each point on the scale is ten times greater than the previous one). Such a drop has not been seen for more than 20 million years. If carbon dioxide emissions continue at present rates, ocean pH is predicted to drop to 7.7 by 2100 and 7.4 by 2300. It has never dropped below 7.5 before. Speaking to *New Scientist* magazine in September 2003, University of Chicago global carbon cycle expert David Archer warned: 'We are taking the reins of the geochemical cycles of the Earth ... It's really frightening.'

What will happen if the ocean acidifies?

Increased acidity reduces the availability of calcium carbonate in seawater, which could have a devastating impact on the many marine organisms that extract calcium carbonate to create their shells or other hard structures, including corals, shellfish, tubeworms, algae, sea urchin and many forms of plankton. Britain's Royal Society also warns that acidification could directly affect the lifecycle of fish, reduce nutrient concentrations in surface waters in some areas, reduce oxygen levels in subsurface waters and increase the exposure of phytoplankton to sunlight. The combined effect of these changes is hard to predict, but in tandem with global warming it is feared that they could severely damage the ocean ecosystem.

Coral reefs

Among the most endangered ocean habitats are coral reefs. Coral polyps stop growing when water temperature exceeds their tolerance range, and raised acidity prevents them from forming new coral. Often described as 'the rainforests of the sea', coral reefs are biodiversity hotspots that also play an important role in the wider ocean ecosystem as fish nurseries. They help to protect shorelines from storms and erosion, and draw vital tourist dollars. In the Caribbean, for instance, it was estimated that in 2000 coral reefs provided goods and services worth up to $4 billion to some of the poorest countries in the northern hemisphere.

On top of the dangers of acidification and warming, coral reefs also have to contend with numerous other threats, including destructive human activities (such as dynamite and cyanide fishing, and insensitive tourism and mining), sediment deposition from rivers and new diseases affecting corals. Scientists estimate that if current trends continue, all of the world's corals may vanish by 2065. Professor Jonathan Erez of the Hebrew University of Jerusalem warned BBC's *Newsnight*: 'As an ecosystem, our grandchildren will not see coral reefs any more.'

Has it happened before?

Ocean pH has fluctuated throughout geological history in response to changing levels of atmospheric carbon dioxide, but the levels of acidity that could occur by 2100 are unprecedented for at least 30 million years – 400 million years according to some experts. In the past, ocean pH has been buffered by carbonate rocks on the ocean floor, which react to more acidic water to soak up the acidity and thus help to prevent the pH from dropping too low. The difference today is that atmospheric CO_2 levels are rising much more quickly than at any time in the past, so that these natural buffering processes, which operate on timescales of 10,000 years, will not have time to respond. Neither will marine species, which are unlikely to be able to adapt quickly enough to cope with such a fundamental change to their environment.

How likely is it to happen?

Disturbingly, a 2003 NASA study suggests that the ocean is already feeling the effects of acidification. Satellite measurements of chlorophyll levels in the ocean show that global ocean productivity seems to have fallen by 6 per cent since the 1980s. Research by the British Antarctic Survey shows that krill, a shrimp-like organism that forms one of the pillars of the Antarctic marine food chain, has declined by up to 80 per cent since the 1970s. And the evidence shows that the world's coral reefs are disappearing at an alarming rate. About a third have already been damaged, and under current trends half of the remaining reefs will disappear by 2030. In the Caribbean, 80 per cent of hard coral has disappeared in the last 30 years and nearly two thirds of remaining reefs are under severe threat from human activities, while in areas of the Maldives and Seychelles there is 99 per cent mortality of corals. These findings also tie in with Debbie MacKenzie's starving ocean hypothesis.

Likelihood: 4
Damage: 6
Fear factor: 5

Death of the wild

The fossil record tells us that there have been five great waves of extinctions in geological history. Today, we may be on the verge of a sixth, for which mankind is directly responsible. For not only are we damaging ourselves and the parts of the environment we use directly, we are also endangering the 'wild' environment that supports the world's other species. Human activities threaten to cause wholesale destruction or degradation of habitats and reduction or extinction of plants and animals. The species and the habitats they make up are collectively referred to as 'biodiversity'.

What will happen if we destroy biodiversity?

Why should we care what happens to biodiversity? Does it really matter if there is less rainforest, or if an obscure species of newt is endangered? There are compelling moral and aesthetic arguments for preserving biodiversity, such as a duty of stewardship for future generations, or giving your grandchildren the chance to see a coral reef, but more pressing than these is the utilitarian argument, which centres on ecosystem services and the direct economic value of biodiversity.

Economic value of biodiversity

Some habitats are so valuable that they are effectively mined for their raw materials – primarily the forests and the oceans. From these we get wood, paper, seafood and many other products. Billions of people in the developing world rely on forests for firewood and building materials. Wild habitats are also vital sources of food for millions. The majority of medicines either come directly or were developed from natural sources, which also offer some of the most exciting prospects for new drugs in many fields. Genetic diversity is also a valuable resource. For instance, many current crop varieties are hybrids created using genes from wild varieties, but much of the world's genetic potential has never even been surveyed.

Ecosystem services

Ecosystem services are important environmental jobs on which our prosperity and survival depend. According to one estimate, the Earth provides services worth over $33 trillion a year, almost twice the total gross product of the world economy. We literally cannot afford to lose these services.

Important ecosystem services already mentioned include: watershed protection; maintenance and regulation of water supplies; soil formation and protection against erosion; maintenance of soil fertility through nitrogen fixing, breakdown of organic material and recycling of nutrients; and storage and mobilisation of nutrients. Other important services include: pollination of plants (including many commercial species, which often cannot be pollinated in any other way); seed dispersal; air filtering and water purification on a global scale; and climate regulation. Forests, in particular, provide a massive carbon sink – a standing forest can contain up to 30,000 tonnes of carbon per square kilometre. They also help to actually generate rainfall through the mechanism of transpiration, whereby moisture is transferred from the soil to the air.

Habitats such as coastal mangrove forests, wetlands and coral reefs can protect humans against natural disasters such as floods or tsunamis, as was graphically demonstrated during the 2004 Boxing Day tsunami disaster, when coastal areas where mangrove forests had been destroyed to make way for shrimp farms suffered far more damage than mangrove-protected areas. Wild habitats also provide homes for the majority of the world's species. Tropical forests, for instance, cover just 6 per cent of the Earth's surface but are home to 50–80 per cent of all plant and animal species, while mangrove swamps and coral reefs are vital nurseries for ocean fish populations including many commercially fished species.

The web of life

There are many possible analogies for the global ecosystem. It's like a complex machine that can be brought grinding to a halt by a single missing bolt, or a house of cards that can be brought crashing down by removing a single one. They serve to illustrate that a complex ecosystem depends on a web of relationships between many elements, and that disturbing that web by removing any of the elements could have unforeseen and disastrous consequences. This is one important argument for trying to preserve global biodiversity – if we lose elements, we simply don't know what effect this will have on the wider ecosystem. Since humanity and the many cultivated species on which we depend are part of this system, it is obvious that we should care what happens to biodiversity, and that we need to protect it.

Has it happened before?

Destruction of wild habitats and species has been a major contributor to collapses of societies in all parts of the world, mainly through deforestation. A classic example is Easter Island in the Pacific. When European explorers came upon Easter Island in the 18th century they found it to be a barren wasteland completely devoid of trees, with only a few species of plants and animals. However, archaeological and sediment evidence shows that it once supported a rich subtropical forest teeming with different species. Short-sighted over-exploitation of the forests, coupled with other causes such as over-hunting and damage inflicted by introduced rats, led to a sequence of total deforestation, the collapse of the island's ecosystem and the subsequent collapse of Easter Island society.

How likely is it to happen?

The major threat to biodiversity comes from the degradation and destruction of whole habitats, and from the pressures driving many species to the brink of extinction.

Forests

Human activity over thousands of years has cleared more than half of the world's original forest cover. Half of that has been lost during the last 50 years, and at current rates of deforestation a quarter of the remaining forests will be gone within the next 50 years. Much of what remains has been seriously degraded. Among the worst hit areas are the tropical rainforests. At current rates of logging and abuse, less than 5 per cent of the Amazon will remain in a pristine state by 2020. Less than 7 per cent of South America's Atlantic rainforest is left. A fifth of Central Africa's rainforest will be gone within 15 years, as they are shrinking at the rate of

8,000 square kilometres per year. Most lowland forests in Indonesia have already disappeared. In total, forests have been almost completely eradicated from 25 countries, and in another 29 the area covered by forest has fallen by more than 90 per cent. Only 12 per cent of the world's forests are protected, and often this protection is purely theoretical, thanks to corruption and lax enforcement.

The causes of deforestation include land clearance to make way for grazing and crops, and use of trees for firewood and building materials. The biggest contributor, however, is destructive logging. Forests can be logged in a sustainable fashion, but this requires care and effort and yields lower short-term returns. Instead, many of the world's forests have been subject to what Jared Diamond calls 'rape-and-run' logging, where companies gain access to a patch of forest, either legally or illegally, cut down and haul off as much as possible and then move on. Legitimate logging companies are less likely to engage in this kind of short-sighted exploitation these days, but illegal loggers have no such scruples. In Indonesia, for instance, 70 per cent of all logging is illegal, and senior government officials there openly admit they are powerless to overcome the corruption involved. Logging is often only the first step in a chain reaction of exploitation: once roads have been cut through a forest, miners, farmers and others can gain access.

There have been some efforts to curb the ravages of unsustainable logging with the establishment of the Forestry Stewardship Council (FSC), precursor to the Marine Stewardship Council, which offers certification to products made from sustainable logging and processing. The FSC has been successful to a limited extent, but even in the UK – the country with the highest rate of FSC certification – only 20 per cent of timber products are certified. Recent UK-led attempts to develop a forceful international initiative along similar lines to the FSC were scuppered by US intransigence, probably linked to industry lobbyists. It is also the case, as US negotiators pointed out, that policy changes are needed in China, which imports a very large proportion of the world's illegal timber, if global action is to have any effect. Similar scepticism can be levelled at a February 2005 treaty aimed at protecting Central African rainforests and signed by leaders of seven nations in a region crippled by corruption, war and inability to enforce conservation.

In summary, the outlook for many of the world's remaining forests, particularly the tropical forests, is bleak, with some of the world's poorest countries either already deforested or facing a treeless future.

Other land habitats

The world's wetlands are under greater threat than its forests. More than 40 per cent have already been lost, while a March 2005 UN report warns that a global temperature rise of 3–4°C (well within the realm of possibility according to many climate scientists) would wipe out 85 per cent of the remaining wetlands. The same report focuses on the immediate threats to the world's largest remaining area of wetland, the Pantanal in South America, and warns that it could easily go the same way as Florida's Everglades, which have shrunk to just a fifth of their original size. The US government is spending $8 billion to try to repair some of the damage.

Grasslands are also in full-scale retreat. Over a quarter of the world's natural grasslands have already been lost, and more has been degraded by overgrazing, poor water management, etc. For instance, over 90 per cent of China's vast natural grasslands are now degraded.

Pollution

Humans aren't the only animals that suffer adverse effects from pollution. Usually it is natural habitats and wild species that take the brunt. Apart from the threat of eutrophication, animals and plants are also in danger from massive use of pesticides (including insecticides and herbicides), oil spills and leaks from mining. These take a fearful toll on the natural world.

Pesticides

Almost all pesticides kill off insects and non-crop plants indiscriminately, creating a vicious cycle where natural predators/limiters of pest growth are removed, so that crops become more vulnerable to pests and so more pesticide is needed. But pesticides don't only harm pests. The consequences for ecosystems can be severe, as powerfully highlighted in Rachel Carson's seminal 1962 book *Silent Spring*. The basic problem is that most pesticides are toxic not only to pests but to all other animals, and that they persist in the environment. This means that they will tend to become concentrated up the food chain, reaching high enough levels to poison even large animals, including humans. So ecosystems suffer at all levels. Insects and other invertebrates – which are vital for soil health, plant pollination and maintaining the balance of an ecosystem – are killed, and so are bigger animals higher up the food chain. Thus pesticide use has knock-on effects for biodiversity, soil fertility and agriculture. Eventually human health is threatened by eating these animals.

Ecocide

Oil Spills

An estimated 0.1 per cent of the oil shipped around the globe each year is spilt into the sea – that's around 2.2 million tonnes of oil per year. The *Exxon Valdez* spill in Alaska devastated 1,500 miles of shoreline but was just an eighth the size of the biggest oil tanker spill of all time, which was the loss of nearly 280,000 tonnes of oil when the *Atlantic Empress* collided with the *Aegean Captain* off the coast of Tobago on 19 July 1979. More recently, in 2002, the *Prestige* oil tanker sank off the coast of Spain and polluted about 1,800 miles of coastline, killing an estimated 300,000 birds. Such tanker disasters are dwarfed by the deliberate release of over 800,000 tonnes of oil from Kuwaiti wells by the Iraqi army in 1991. Clean-up operations can remove much of the surface spillage, but a lot of the oil sinks to the sea bottom and lurks there, seeping toxic molecules into the food chains for decades. The *Prestige* spill, for instance, is probably still polluting a heavily exploited fishery.

Leaks from mines

Leaks from mines also release potentially deadly poisons into rivers and oceans. The main threat is posed by storage lakes, where slurry from mines and water used in extraction processes – often heavily contaminated with poisons such as arsenic and sulphuric acid – is held in place by poorly maintained dams. When these inevitably fail, they release a sudden burst of toxins into the environment. On average there is one major storage lake accident per year. For instance, in 2000 the storage pond at a gold mine in Baia Mare, Romania, burst its banks and released 100 tonnes of cyanide into rivers, wiping out all fish and plant life for hundreds of miles. Two years later fish catches in the rivers were still only a fifth of former levels. In the future there will be probably be an increasing frequency of such events, as the incidence of heavy rainstorms and flooding increases due to climate change and deforestation.

Disappearing species

Many scientists believe that human activities are as destructive as the huge asteroid strikes that caused past mass extinctions. According to the 2005 Millennium Ecosystem Assessment – a four-year multinational intergovernmental project – the current rate of extinctions is between 100 and 1,000 times the natural background rate of extinctions, and 10–30 per cent of the world's mammal, bird and amphibian species are under threat of extinction. Many more species have been drastically reduced in numbers and range.

Primary causes include habitat destruction, climate change, pollution and hunting and poaching. Hunting and poaching are thought to be behind the recently revealed disappearance of most of India's tigers, widely regarded as emblematic of the global threat to biodiversity. Despite a high profile, 20-year campaign of conservation linked to a series of parks and reserves, it is now believed that poaching, coupled with official corruption and incompetence, has probably destroyed all but a few hundred of the country's tigers, leaving the remaining populations on the edge of viability. Most of the poaching is directed at supplying China's traditional medicine market. The same market is linked to poaching and unsustainable hunting in many parts of the world. As Chinese affluence increases, and access to Chinese markets improves, this issue is expected to get worse.

Alien invaders

Another major cause of biodiversity loss is alien species – the introduction of organisms that are not indigenous to an area. Significant examples include: Dutch elm disease, which wiped out almost the entire elm tree population of Britain; lamprey infestations in the Great Lakes, which have destroyed previously productive fisheries; and the cane toad invasion of Australia, where toxic toads, introduced as a form of pest control but which proved fatal to indigenous wildlife, are advancing across the country at a rate of 50 kilometres (30 miles) a year and now infest 100,000 square kilometres.

The outlook for biodiversity

Many, if not most, of the causes underlying loss of biodiversity seem to be getting worse, not better. With even high profile, well-supported efforts such as the Indian tiger programme in jeopardy, it is hard to be optimistic about the prospects for con-servation. Future ecological pressures on humans are likely to bring even greater pressure on biodiversity, as man squeezes the global ecosystem to make up for shortfalls in water, land and other resources. Whether loss of biodiversity could threat-en civilisation depends on the unpredictable consequences of disturbing the 'web of life'. The probable result will simply be declining quality of life and rising costs as ecosystems become impoverished and can no longer provide ecosystem services. However, there is the possibility of a dramatic collapse that completely overturns fundamental geochemical cycles such as the carbon cycle, with catastrophic consequences for mankind (see 'Waking the giants', Chapter 4).

Likelihood: 7
Damage: 7
Fear factor: 7

The aspiration bomb

During the 1970s the main prophets of doom for civilisation concentrated on population growth as the likely agent of destruction. Led by Stanford University professor Paul Ehrlich and his 1968 book *The Population Bomb*, they predicted that the massive increase in global population over the coming decades would not be matched by food production. In practice, advances in agriculture and the world economy have allowed the world to sustain a much bigger population, and give confidence that it will be able to do so into the future. The latest UN estimates predict that world population will rise from 6.5 billion today to 9.1 billion by 2050. It is also the case that the rate of growth of population does seem to be gradually tailing off – thanks to prosperity, female education, population control policies and declining fertility rates (which may be linked to pollution) – so that world population will reach a ceiling of around 10 billion.

The failure of these past doomsday prophecies caused a backlash against predictions of a population crisis, and generated considerable optimism about the future. On some levels this optimism seems well founded. Many experts agree that the world could provide 10 billion people with enough food and other resources to meet their basic needs. There would be a serious toll on the environment, with less space and resources for 'wild' habitats and species, but it could be done. So where is the problem? Are the doomsday sceptics right to dismiss population size as a cause for concern?

The real problem with population is not simply the number of people, but their ecological 'footprints'. A person's ecological footprint is the impact that he or she has on the environment. It is a function of the resources they consume and the waste they generate. People in the developed world have much bigger footprints than those in the developing world. Per capita, they consume more food, water and energy, and generate more pollution – 32 times more, according to Jared Diamond. The problem, then, is one of aspiration. People in the developing world (quite reasonably) aspire to developed world living standards, with the corresponding footprints, while people in the developed world aspire to maintain their living standards (and footprints) at the very least.

What will happen if the aspiration bomb goes off?

Diamond estimates that if the entire population of the developing world increased their living standards to developed world levels, it would increase their impact on the global ecosystem by a factor of 12. Even if this process were restricted to the population of China, human impact on the environment would double. This is clearly not sustainable.

Has it happened before?

World population was drastically smaller just a few decades ago, as were average ecological footprints in the developed world. The combination of massive population growth with massive increase in living standards is unprecedented in human history. Nonetheless, a few grisly episodes in human history offer some insight into what happens when more and more people try to grab a slice of a cake that doesn't increase in size to keep pace. The most obvious examples are the genocides perpetrated by colonists against indigenous peoples, which have occurred throughout human history (eg the European colonisation of North America and Australia). In such instances, the standard of living desired by colonists left insufficient resources for the indigenous peoples, and conflict and destruction ensued. More recently, the 1994 genocide in Rwanda may have been driven by over-population leading to tension over dwindling resources (particularly land).

How likely is it to happen?

At the moment the proportion of the world's population with large ecological footprints is relatively small. If this state of affairs remained stable over the next few decades, the 3 billion increase in world population might be manageable. But it is already changing fast, as people either migrate to the developed world or increase their standard of living in the developing world. Meanwhile, constant growth is the primary aim of government policy around the world and the cornerstone of the global economy. Any government or organisation that tries to burst the aspiration bubble will fail. Are voters in America or Europe likely to elect a party that promises to reduce living standards? How can the developed world tell the developing world to drop their aspirations?

Some commentators argue that economic development and raised living standards are the key to solving environmental problems – only rich societies can afford to conserve habitats, safeguard resources, farm sustainably and dispose of waste responsibly. But ultimately this wealth must come from somewhere, so even if you accept this argument (and many argue the opposite – ie that ecological degradation causes poverty) it is hard to see how the global environment can supply enough for everyone.

Likelihood: 8
Damage: 7
Fear factor: 7

Conclusion: Overshoot and ecocide

Over millions of years the Earth has built up a vast amount of ecological capital, in terms of its natural resources – from clean air and water to fertile soils and diverse ecosystems. Since the advent of farming and the start of civilisation, mankind has been spending that ecological capital. Natural processes and systems steadily replenish spent capital, but can the pace of this replenishment compete with the accelerating rate of spending by mankind since industrialisation? If expenditure outstrips income, bankruptcy must be the inevitable result. The sheer quantity of ecological capital on Earth has made this result difficult to envisage, but the evidence, detailed in this chapter, is that we are indeed spending faster than the Earth can replenish. According to Sir Crispin Tickell, of Oxford University's Green College Centre for Environmental Policy and Understanding, 'The ecological overshoot could have been as much as 20 per cent of supply by the beginning of this century [ie 2000].'

The Millennium Ecosystem Assessment was devised specifically to analyse and quantify this ecological overshoot, and its findings make grim reading. Its main conclusion is that approximately 60 per cent of the planet's ecosystem services are being degraded or used unsustainably, increasing the risk of sudden and catastrophic changes, such as the collapse of fisheries or climate change. These problems are likely to be magnified by population and economic growth.

The Millennium Ecosystem Assessment is supposed to provide direction and frameworks for no less than four international treaties on environmental issues (including the UN Convention on Biological Diversity) but some environmentalists are sceptical, arguing that there is no clear mechanism for this to happen. Even optimists admit that the Millennium Ecosystem Assessment is just the first step in a long process that could take a decade or more to feed through into policy. Will this be too little, too late? What will happen if urgent action is deferred by a decade?

Outcomes

Some of the possible outcomes of all this ecological damage have been discussed above. It is very likely, for instance, that food prices will rise dramatically to reflect the true (environmental) cost of production, and the same may go for most other products. This is likely to reduce standards of living in the developed world and threaten food security in the developing world. Widespread famine might result. Whether or not this would constitute a threat to civilisation is uncertain, but it would certainly increase the risk of mass immigration, terrorism inspired by injustice and resentment and conflict over resources (such as water).

More alarming is the prospect that human activity will cause a complete ecological meltdown: ecocide. In this scenario mass extinctions coincide with dramatically reduced productivity to leave large swathes of the planet barren, dramatically impoverished or inhabited only by pest species. Provision of ecosystem services collapses entirely, so that there is little or no natural recycling of elements, breakdown of wastes, replenishment of soil fertility or purification of air and water. Crops fail and livestock die. Rainfall patterns alter and droughts hit vital crop-producing areas. There is massive erosion and desertification. Pollution and rubbish accumulate, with severe consequences for human health. Changes to global geochemical cycles could set off massive climate changes. Ecocide would almost certainly end global civilisation in its present form, killing billions and setting back the clock to give the sort of *Mad Max* scenario described at the start of this chapter, where a hi-tech, affluent minority retreat into biodomes of the sort beloved of sci-fi authors, and the rest of the survivors struggle to maintain a short, brutish life.

Even if this extreme ecocide scenario seems far-fetched, the chances that ecological overshoot will severely dent our current standards of living must rate as high to very high, making it the most serious threat to civilisation covered in this book.

Chapter 4
Climate Change

It is the year 2055. The storm season, a time of hurricane winds lashing huge storm surges far up the drowned valleys, has finally given way to the relentless, blazing heat of summer. As the mercury climbs above 40ºc for the ninth day in succession, the boatload of emaciated migrants noses between the sunken buildings, trying to find the main course of the river. This year's surges have pushed the water beyond the makeshift flood defences of the inner city parks. The rotting vegetation in the stagnant water gives off a foul smell, and the captain growls a warning to his human cargo: no naked flames. The men leaning over the side pay scant notice; their attention is fixed on the search for food. One of them spots a movement and calls out. The net is cast, and heaved in with satisfaction to reveal a fat, slimy rat, one of the few animals that can survive in the oxygen-free, silt-choked, garbage-clogged waters.

As the boat leaves the drowned centre of the old capital and the sun climbs in the sky, pushing the temperature still higher, the passengers catch their first sight of the lands they have travelled so far to find. A murmur of dismay rises from the crowd – the scene is little different from the country they fled. Scrub and pines cover the hills where woods of beech and oak once stood, and bare, dusty patches scarred with deep gullies show where hopeless optimists struggled to farm. Most of the houses, distorted into crazy angles by the sagging ground, are abandoned. The only structures teeming with life are the termite mounds rising incongruously between the empty suburban homes. Ahead, the migrants hope, lie more welcoming lands, but to reach them they must somehow evade the border patrols, breach the security cordon and avoid the attentions of the Vigilance Committee. They should be afraid, but with nothing to lose they have no reason to turn back. What lies ahead cannot be worse than what they have left behind.

Future climates

This scenario, with its heatwaves, wild weather, rising sea levels and shifting habitats, is just one of the outcomes feared by those who argue that the global climate will change disastrously unless we take action. Other gloomy prognoses include a new Ice Age or even global suffocation due to mass release of methane. In addition, there are many climate change sceptics who argue that climate change is not happening, or that climate change is an entirely natural process that cannot be affected for better or worse by human activities. So is climate change inevitable, and if so, how worried should we be? This chapter investigates several different climate change scenarios, but concentrates mainly on the complex issues of global warming caused by human activities.

Global warming

Global warming is hard to avoid. There are constant references to it in the media, and the evidence of unseasonal weather, early spring flowering and summer heatwaves seems to be all around us. But as familiar as terms like 'global warming' and 'greenhouse effect' may be, do you really know what they mean?

The science of global warming

The Earth gets some heat from the radioactive decay of elements in the core, but the surface is mainly warmed by radiation from the Sun. When solar radiation hits the Earth some of it is reflected or absorbed by the top of the atmosphere (for example, the ozone layer screens out most of the harmful UV radiation) and some by clouds in the lower atmosphere. The rest of it hits the surface of the Earth, where, again, it is reflected or absorbed. When the ground or sea absorbs solar radiation it heats up and radiates most of this heat back as infrared radiation, which has a longer wavelength than the incoming solar radiation. On a planet like Mars, with a thin atmosphere, most of this heat radiates back out into space and the surface remains very cold. On Earth, however, the presence of a thick atmosphere causes what is called the greenhouse effect.

The greenhouse effect
Gases in the atmosphere, particularly water vapour, carbon dioxide, methane and nitrous oxide, which are transparent to the short wavelengths of solar radiation, are not transparent to the longer wavelengths of heat radiation. They act like the

panes of glass in a greenhouse, allowing energy in but not letting it escape (hence they are known as greenhouse gases). The effect is to maintain the atmosphere and surface of the Earth at a much higher temperature than would be the case if there were no atmosphere. In fact, without the greenhouse effect the average surface temperature would be -18°C, and life as we know it would never have evolved. The higher the level of greenhouse gases in the atmosphere, the greater the greenhouse effect and so the higher the surface temperature and atmospheric temperature will become. The concern today is that the planet is undergoing anthropogenic (human-caused) warming, mainly as the result of massive emissions of greenhouse gases.

What will happen if the world heats up?

If global warming is already underway, what should we expect? Will the consequences of warming threaten civilisation? The list of potential impacts is disturbing.

How hot will it get?

This depends mainly on how high levels of carbon dioxide get, and on how the various feedback loops that influence global climate respond. The main international body on climate warning, the Intergovernmental Panel on Climate Change (IPCC), synthesises the work of thousands of researchers and dozens of models to come up with predictions. Assuming that atmospheric CO_2 levels can be stabilised at around twice pre-industrial levels – ie around 560 parts per million – which most environmentalists think is optimistic at best, the IPCC predicts warming of between 1.4 and 5.8°C by 2100. The upper limit of this range is more than the difference between the last Ice Age and today, while even the lower end of the range would be the biggest temperature change in the entire history of civilisation. The general consensus is that mankind needs to avoid a rise of more than 2°C to avoid the worst consequences of global warming.

IPCC predictions represent a fairly conservative consensus by the main body of climate scientists who do not wish to be alarmist. But the results of a recent study that compared thousands of possible models using millions of computers suggest that the IPCC has been far too conservative, and that temperatures will rise by at least 2°C and possibly as much as 11°C over the next century.

All of these models have wide margins of variation. This is because there are so many unknowns surrounding feedback loops that could limit or accelerate global warming.

Changing climatic regimes

Temperature will not increase evenly across the board. Models suggest that the biggest rises will affect the polar regions and much of the northern land masses, as well as areas that are already hot, such as the Sahara and Australia.

Changing temperatures will lead to changing climatic regimes. Semi-arid areas will become deserts. Temperate areas may develop Mediterranean or chaparral climates. This will have serious effects for agriculture around the world; some areas will experience benefits, but it would be a mistake to think that the positives will balance out the negatives. The most populous regions are likely to be the most adversely affected. For instance, a report by the European Climate

Forum predicts that a temperature rise of 2.5–3°C could reduce rice yield in China by a fifth. Agriculture in Southern Asia could be even worse hit. It could be hard to increase global food production to make up these losses because the areas that are likely to 'benefit' from higher temperatures may not be particularly productive, owing to poor water resources, poor soils and weak sunlight at higher latitudes.

Climate change could be too rapid for habitats to adapt to, causing massive die-off of plants with little replacement growth. For instance, warming could lead to drying in the Amazon region, with some models predicting that it could dry out and burn by 2050, releasing its carbon into the atmosphere.

Climatic regime change could have serious geopolitical consequences, reinforcing the North–South/First World–Third World divisions that developing nations such as China, India and Brazil are just beginning to overcome. There might be an increase in the relative power/influence of countries such as Canada and Russia, which stand to suffer fewer negative climatic consequences than the rest of the world. More obviously, the impact of global warming on the food crisis is likely to increase tension and the potential for conflict in most parts of the world.

Heatwaves

A severe heatwave in Europe in 2003 is thought to have cost around 15,000 lives. Many climate experts are warning that such waves could become much more common and extreme. According to modelling by the US National Center for Atmospheric Research (NCAR), the frequency of heatwaves in France, for instance, is likely to increase by 31 per cent over the next 100 years, and the waves are likely to last up to 50 per cent longer. The UK's Hadley Centre for Climate Prediction and Research estimates that human-caused emissions have already doubled the risk of 2003-type heatwaves, while another study suggests that at current rates of greenhouse gas emission similar heatwaves will occur every other year. Though short-lived, such extreme weather events could prove to be the biggest global warming killer in the developed world, and could also produce unexpected consequences for infrastructure – eg rapid changes in the water table owing to short, sharp droughts could affect the foundations of houses, or high temperatures could melt tarmac and cause rails to buckle, crippling transport.

Changing rainfall patterns

The biggest global warming killer in the developing world could prove to be drought, as rising temperatures cause disastrous changes in rainfall patterns, such as weakening the Asian monsoon or intensifying the Pacific weather phenomenon known as El Niño.

The risk of drought is ironic, because global warming is likely to cause more evaporation, more water vapour in the air and therefore more precipitation. But experts predict that more and more rain will fall in 'useless' fashion as heavy storms causing flooding and erosion. Rain that falls in heavy bursts or storms is much more likely to be lost as run-off into rivers and oceans, rather than gradually seeping into the earth to replenish groundwater stocks and reservoirs, and it is also more likely to cause damage, erosion and flooding.

Heavier rain leading to flooding is likely to become an issue all over the world. In Europe, for instance, climate forecasters warn that once-in-a-thousand-year flood events – such as those that hit Central Europe in August 2002, forcing the evacuation of hundreds of thousands of people – could become far more common. People who live on marginal land on or next to steep slopes will be at risk of landslides and mudslides, a risk exacerbated by deforestation; incidence of these events is already increasing around the world. Richard Betts from the Hadley Centre warns that elevated CO_2 levels stimulate plants to shrink their stomata (the tiny holes in the leaves through which they transpire water vapour). This would cut down water evaporation from plants and by extension from the soil, increasing groundwater levels by 10 per cent (10 times more than warming-linked rainfall), according to current emissions forecasts. This is enough to massively increase flooding, slides and soil erosion. Slides and erosion will also increase because of melting permafrost, which destabilises previously solid soil and rock.

Disappearing glaciers

Warming threatens to melt important glacial water reserves. Some of the world's largest rivers – including the Ganges, Indus, Brahmaputra, Mekong and Yellow rivers – depend on meltwater from glaciers to regulate flow and keep the rivers going during dry months. In South America many communities in arid regions along the Andes depend almost entirely on glacial meltwater. Even in North America many arid areas, such as California and Montana, depend on snow and glacier melt. But the rapid and accelerating retreat of glaciers in many parts of the world threatens to expose these communities first to floods, and then to droughts. The Gangorti glacier at the head of the Ganges, for instance, is retreating at 30 metres a year. According to the WWF, rises in global mean temperatures of just 2ºC could devastate vulnerable communities in India, Nepal, Bangladesh and China. These areas are already showing signs of climate change-related water scarcity, such as empty rivers and dry wetlands. Similar consequences can be expected in South America and other areas that depend on glacial melt-water. Disappearing snow caps and glaciers also mean that winter sports may soon be a thing of the past.

Rising sea levels

The IPCC predicts that unless emissions are drastically curbed, melting of the ice caps could cause sea levels to rise by anywhere from 9 to 88 centimetres by 2100. This is a very wide margin of uncertainty, and many climate scientists fear that the lower estimate is highly conservative. If the upper estimate proves more accurate, many major cities would be at grave risk from flooding, including New York, London, Tokyo, Sydney and New Orleans, together with much of the most densely populated land in the world, such as the Netherlands, Bangladesh, the eastern US, Nile and Mekong deltas. For instance, at least a fifth of Bangladesh, one of the most dense-ly populated countries in the world, would be under water.

The hardest hit will be island nations that are entirely at or near sea level, which may simply vanish by the end of the century. For instance, 80 per cent of the islands of the Maldives, home to 370,000 people, are less than 1 metre above sea level – the upper end of the IPCC estimate will see them vanish by 2100.

Higher sea levels will be compounded by storm surges. Storms are set to become stronger and more frequent as global warming boosts the amount of energy in the atmosphere.

For instance, by 2080 in the southern North Sea, what are currently considered 150-year storms could occur every 7–8 years, causing storm surges up to 1.2 metres higher than today with devastating consequence for vast tracts of eastern England.

Elevated sea levels and increased flooding would make millions homeless and devastate economies through damage to property, loss of livelihoods, damage to infrastructure and industry, and damage to farmland. In London, for example, at least £80 billion worth of property will be at risk of flooding by 2100 if mid-high IPCC estimates are accurate. Global trade could be disrupted by drowning of ports. Rising sea levels would threaten food security by swamping some of the world's most productive land and leaching salt into unflooded soils. Water security would also be threatened by the rising sea levels contaminating drinking and irrigation water with salt.

Toxic pollution from flooded urban, industrial and agricultural land would pour directly into the sea. Flooded habitats would rot to give off methane, while large areas of shallow, stagnant water would increase the risk of disease, especially from insects. Biodiversity would also suffer as coastal habitats would change faster than species can adapt. Beaches, mudflats, marshes and other important habitats would be swamped, together with mammal and bird breeding colonies. And newly created coastal zones would be made inhospitable by pollution, sediment and debris.

How high could sea levels get?

If the polar ice caps melted completely sea levels would rise by 115 metres or more. Admittedly, it would take hundreds or even thousands of years for them to melt completely, but once the 'big melt' starts it is likely to be a self-reinforcing process –

a positive feedback loop that can only be reversed by a new Ice Age. Some scientists fear that conditions for triggering this loop are already in place. The UK government's top scientific advisor Professor Sir David King points out that CO_2 levels are already nearly at the same level as 55 million years ago, when there was no ice on the planet. According to Hadley Centre experts, an average global temperature rise of just 1.5°C (within most projected ranges) would cause local warming of 2.7°C over Greenland, enough to trigger the irreversible melting of the Greenland ice cap and raise sea levels by 7 metres.

Natural disasters

Global warming is expected to increase the incidence of floods, landslides, mudslides, storms and storm surges, but incredibly it could also trigger major geophysical catastrophes. Explosive release of methane sediments in continental shelf areas (which is considered a distinct possibility) might trigger huge submarine landslides, which in turn would set off mega-tsunami (see Chapter 5). It is believed that the Storegga Slides – massive submarine landslides off the coast of Norway 7,000 years ago – triggered mega-tsunami in this way, leaving sandy deposits in peat high up on Scottish hillsides. The sheer weight of water on continental margins from rising sea levels could even trigger volcanoes and earthquakes (again, this is thought to have happened in the past).

Ozone holes

Most people assume that the ozone holes – a thinning of the ozone layer over the polar regions, which lets through more harmful ultraviolet radiation from the Sun – are under control.

But more greenhouse gases will trap more heat in the lower atmosphere, leaving the upper atmosphere cooler, which in turn may increase the size of the ozone holes. If the Arctic hole gets big enough, heavily populated areas of the Europe and North America could get blasted by high levels of UV radiation.

Extinctions

Evolution is a slow process, so many species would not be able to adapt to the rapid pace of the climate change predicted. Previous major climate changes have either been linked to mass extinctions, or have seen biodiversity maintained by retreat to a few habitat reservoirs – eg patches of rainforest that survive dry conditions because they are nestled in deep valleys. This will be less of an option in the industrial era, because of competition for land and space with the large and growing human population. In fact, human response to climate change may be as much of a threat to biodiversity as climate change itself. Human populations under pressure are more likely to out-compete other species for diminishing resources such as water, dry land, firewood, etc.

Alien invaders

Alien species are already a major problem for agriculture and indigenous species in many parts of the world (see Chapter 3). Climate change is likely to increase the scale of this problem by allowing tropical species to move into previously temperate zones. It may also favour pest species, because they tend to be more adaptable and can cope better with environmental stress. Among the potential unwelcome arrivals in previously temperate countries, look out for termites, malarial mosquitoes, killer bees, army ants, cockroaches, poisonous spiders and many others.

Has it happened before?

The history of human civilisation has coincided with one of the most stable periods in the climatic history of the Earth, but even within this period there have been shifts dramatic enough to end civilisations or jump-start new ones. In geological history, the Earth has been a sweltering, ice-free hothouse and a completely frozen 'snowball' planet, covered in thick ice down to the equator.

If climate change is nothing new, and levels of greenhouse gases have fluctuated dramatically due to natural causes many times in the past, why should we be anxious? There are two major differences between those prehistoric shifts and climate change today. Firstly, civilisation did not exist at those times. We know that those past climate shifts had serious consequences for life on the planet (causing mass extinctions, for instance). What effect would comparable shifts have on civilisation? Secondly, we know just enough about global cycles, feedback loops and tipping points to worry that human activities could cause dramatic or even runaway changes to climate, but not enough to understand precisely how serious the risks or exactly what the consequences might be.

Ecotones and the rise and fall of the Roman Empire

Historically, even relatively subtle climate changes have ruled the fates of empires. The extension of Roman hegemony over

Western Europe and the eventual decline and fall of Rome, for instance, were closely linked to climatic changes in the centuries around 0 CE.

Prior to the 1st century BCE, the European 'ecotone' (a boundary between two different climatic regimes – in this case, the boundary between the cool-wet-northern climate and the warm-dry-Mediterranean-style climate) was situated roughly at the level of the Mediterranean coast of France/the north of Italy. Not coincidentally, this roughly matched the boundary between the power of Rome and the disparate Celtic tribes of Europe. When the ecotone shifted northwards during the 1st century BCE, the Romans, who were culturally adapted to the warm-dry climatic regime (eg through their agriculture), were able to take advantage and extend their influence across all of Western Europe, as far north as Scotland and Germany. When the ecotone shifted back south a few centuries later the cultural and economic basis of the western Roman Empire was fatally undermined. Meanwhile, related climatic changes were driving massive migrations from Asia to Europe, which in turn displaced the 'barbarian' hordes that eventually overran the Western Empire and Rome itself. Could this prove to be a foreshadowing of a similar mass movement of population from less developed countries to more developed ones weakened by climate change in the near future?

How likely is it to happen?

This is the six-million-dollar question, but the answer is not straightforward. To give a proper response we need to ask several other questions. Is global warming already happening? If so, is it down to human activities or is it an entirely natural process? Do the climate change sceptics have a point? And even if we accept that global warming is happening because of humans, what is the likelihood that we will get our act together to stop or limit it?

What is the evidence that global warming is happening?

If global warming due to a greenhouse effect really was going on already, we would expect to see evidence of it. To be precise, we would expect there to be evidence that temperatures have risen and are still going up; that CO_2 levels have risen and are still rising; and that as a result of rising temperatures ice caps are melting, rainfall patterns are changing, sea levels are rising, the weather is getting wilder and nature is responding. On all these counts the evidence strongly suggests that the world *is* getting warmer.

- *Temperature changes*: Temperature records from the last 140 years show a definite warming trend with average temperatures rising by 0.6°C, with 0.5°C of this having come in the last 30 years. All 19 of the 20 warmest years on record have occurred since 1980, including four out of the last seven. None of these facts are really contested, even by sceptics.

  Information about climate variation over the longer term, before records were kept, is obtained from what are known as 'proxy' sources: ice cores, sediment cores, tree rings and others. These sources seem to show that the last 100 years have seen a sharp rise in temperature after a 900-year period of more or less stable temperatures.

- *Carbon dioxide levels*: Pre-industrial levels of CO_2 in the atmosphere were 280 parts per million, but in 2005 stood at

378 parts per million, according to the US National Oceanic and Atmospheric Administration (NOAA). CO_2 levels have been going up every year since 1958, when NOAA measurements began, and the rate at which they are rising is also accelerating – twice as fast during the last decade as during the 1960s. Alarmingly, the last two years of measurements seem to show that the annual rise has leapt from 1.5 parts per million per year to more than 2 parts per million per year.

• *Melting ice and snow:* According to the international team of scientists behind the 2004 Arctic Climate Impact Assessment, the Arctic is warming at twice the global rate, which is exactly what most of the climate models predict. Temperatures in some parts of Alaska have gone up by 4.4°C in the last 30 years. The extent of Arctic sea ice in spring and summer is now 10–15 per cent smaller than during the 1960s, and it decreased in thickness by 40 per cent between the 1960s and the 90s. Average spring snow cover in the northern hemisphere is 10 per cent less than the 1966–86 average. The other pole is also heating up fast, with some Antarctic glaciers flowing six times faster than 50 years ago because the sea ice that usually holds them back has melted. Average temperatures in the Antarctic Peninsula have rocketed by 2.5°C in the last 50 years, while 87 per cent of glaciers on the Peninsula are shrinking, at an average rate of 50 metres per year. Glaciers in other parts of the world also seem to be in headlong retreat. In the Himalayas, for instance, major glaciers are retreating at between 10 and 15 metres a year.

• *Changing rainfall:* A hotter planet means more evaporation and more water in the atmosphere, which in turn means more precipitation overall. Unfortunately, however, this precipitation is not evenly distributed. Many parts of the world are now experiencing more drought than ever. According to scientists from the US National Center for Atmospheric Research, the fraction of the Earth's land area suffering from drought has more than doubled in the past 30 years. In 2002 some 30 per cent of the world's land surface experienced very dry conditions, up from 15 per cent in 1970. Other parts of the world are experiencing heavier rainfall – in particular, the high latitudes of the northern hemisphere. Flow from Arctic rivers is increasing by 8.73 cubic kilometres per year.

- *Rising sea levels:* Melting ice and thermal expansion (water expands as it heats up) mean rising sea levels. On the northeast coast of England, for instance, sea level is rising by 6 millimetres a year. A quarter of this is due to gradual tilting of Britain after the last Ice Age, but the rest seems to be due to global warming. In Alaska, the sea is advancing by up to 3 metres a year. Globally, sea levels rose by between 10 and 20 centimetres during the 20th century.

- *Wild weather:* According to the leading insurance company Munich Re, 2004 was the most expensive year in history for insurers in terms of paying out for damage from natural disasters, mainly hurricanes. The total cost was over $90 billion. The UN says that 254 million people were affected by natural disasters in 2004 – three times more than in 1990 – with 337 natural disasters reported worldwide, as opposed to 261 in 1990. Most of these were weather-related, such as hurricanes, floods, landslides and droughts, and the increases are generally put down to climate change, exacerbated by environmental degradation.

- *Changing biodiversity.* The characteristics of an ecosystem are to a large extent determined by its climate/temperature, so warming would be expected to cause changes in habitats and species distribution. This does seem to be happening. In Europe, for instance, many plants are blooming or coming into leaf much earlier than in previous years, while new species are establishing themselves – eg new types of spider in Southern England, or great white sharks seen in British waters for the first time. In the Antarctic, populations of krill are declining rapidly, possibly because melting ice is making it harder for them to find food (they feed off algae on the underside of ice floes). In the North Atlantic and North Sea, cold water species of plankton are disappearing and being replaced by warm water species. Dr Martin Edwards, of the Sir Alistair Hardy Foundation for Ocean Science, told the BBC: 'The North Sea was a cold temperate ecosystem in the 1980s, but since the 90s it has changed into a warm temperate ecosystem.' Populations of sea birds such as kittiwakes and fulmar are declining fast, possibly as a result.

Is the warming caused by human activities?

The mass of evidence from different sources is overwhelming, and few serious experts dispute that warming is going on to some extent. What is less clear is whether the warming is part of a natural cycle of climate changes, or is due to human activities and in particular greenhouse gas emissions.

Major climate changes in prehistoric times were clearly not caused by human activities. Instead, they resulted from natural processes, such as changes in the amount of energy given off by the Sun, or cyclic changes in the Earth's orbit and tilt. Couldn't these be responsible for the current warming? There are two main reasons to think that this is not the case. Firstly, as detailed above, carbon dioxide levels in the atmosphere *have* increased sharply since the mid-1800s, and it is widely accepted that this is because of industrial emissions. Secondly, the case for human-caused warming is strongly supported by climate models.

Modelling climate change

The ultimate scientific test to determine whether global warming is being caused by human activities would be to take two planets, one with humans and one without, set them up with identical starting conditions matching the Earth c.1800, and compare their climates after 200 years. In the absence of this *Hitchhiker's Guide* scenario, scientists have to make do with artificial simulations of the Earth and its climate using computer models. By changing the parameters and then running the model, scientists can check which scenario best matches the real world. Almost all of the models that have been created by climate scientists agree that rising CO_2 levels and global warming are the result of human activities.

There are two important recent examples. In February 2005 the US Scripps Institution of Oceanography reported that their model showed that rising ocean temperatures were linked to industrial emissions with a 95 per cent degree of certainty. Perhaps more significantly, a model of what current temperatures would be like if they were purely the result of natural changes, such as solar and volcanic activity, predicts that the Earth would actually have cooled slightly compared to 19th century data. Only if human activities are included in the model do predictions match the actual, observed changes. In other words, far from being responsible for global warming, natural factors may have actually masked or slowed it down.

Will the warming continue?

Many climate change sceptics are willing to accept that there is some global warming going on. What they do not accept is that it will be as bad as the IPCC make out, for a variety of reasons: natural processes that act to limit global warming; the relatively small impact of human activities; and inadequacies in the models used by climate scientists.

Will natural processes act to limit global warming?

Sceptics argue that there may be negative feedback loops built into the global system, which act as buffers, damping out fluctuations to maintain a relatively stable climate. An example of a negative feedback loop is where an increase in factor A causes an increase in factor B, but where factor B in turn causes a decrease in factor A. Sceptics point to negative feedback loops such as absorption of gas by the oceans, plant growth and cloud formation, and argue that the IPCC is being unnecessarily alarmist.

- *Absorption of gas by the ocean:* As water heats up it can absorb more gas, so warming should cause a negative feedback loop as the oceans absorb more greenhouse gases. There is a lot of evidence that the oceans have indeed been absorbing atmospheric carbon dioxide, becoming much more acidic in the process. But models suggest that warming may actually compromise the ability of the oceans to absorb heat: as surface layers heat up quickly there will be less of the mixing between surface and deep layers that transfers heat to the depths. This would dramatically slow heat absorption by the ocean, as well as having knock-on effects on the ocean ecosystem. In other words, the sceptics may be wrong about this.

- *Plant growth*: Higher temperatures and CO_2 concentrations stimulate plant growth, which soaks up CO_2 and thus limits the greenhouse effect. There is evidence that plants are indeed growing faster and helping to buffer climate change at present, but models suggest that in the long term, warming is likely to make vegetation an exacerbating factor rather than a limiting one. Experiments show that as temperatures rise so the rate of decomposition of organic material goes up, until carbon is being released faster than plants are soaking it up. When this happens on a global scale, the planet's plant life will become a net producer of carbon. In other words the sceptics may be wrong about this too.

- *Cloud formation*: If the atmosphere does become wetter more clouds will form. This could have a global dimming effect, or it could increase warming by trapping heat radiated from the ground at night. Clouds are considered to be the largest unknown factor in climate models.

Puny humans

Another argument is that human inputs to the climate system are simply too small to be responsible for the kind of changes expected by the IPCC. For instance, an October 2003 study by Swedish scientists suggested that world oil and gas reserves would run out before enough could be burned to seriously affect the climate. Unfortunately, even if they are right there is more than enough coal to produce dangerous levels of CO_2 emissions. On a broader scale, sceptics point out that while human-caused CO_2 emissions amount to 7 billion tonnes a year, natural emissions from plants and animals and from ocean outgassing (release of dissolved gases into the atmosphere) release 150 billion tonnes a year. Surely the human influence on the system must be negligible? Natural systems have built in feedbacks that should easily be able to buffer such minor fluctuations. This is one of the great unknowns of climate science, but the counter-argument is that while natural release and absorption mechanisms are in balance, man-made emissions are big enough to knock the system out of balance. Research shows that even small wobbles can be enough to tip a system out of balance.

Invalid models
Ultimately the core of the debate comes down to the accuracy of observations and models. Even hardened sceptics are having to admit that the observations about current warming are sound. What is up for grabs is the issue of models. These are by their nature speculative, and sceptics argue that the unknowns and margins of error are so great that models are worthless. However, models are the only route available, and the overwhelming consensus of scientific opinion is that climate modelling is valid and that existing models, while not perfect, are worthwhile.

A real consensus
The sceptics seem to have influence disproportionate to their numbers. A 2004 study by science historian Naomi Oreskes, reported in *New Scientist* magazine, showed that the 928 serious scientific papers on climate change published between 1993 and 2003 gave an almost universal consensus about the science of global warming. She concludes:

> *Politicians, economists, journalists and others may have the impression of confusion, disagreement or discord among climate scientists, but that impression is incorrect.*

So why do politicians, journalists and much of the public have an impression of confusion and discord? Sceptics are well-funded (often by oil companies) and have friends in high places, particularly in American politics where the vested interests of the fossil fuel business are strong. But they are also helped by the way the media works. In seeking to be seen to give a balanced account of issues, the media follows a well-worn format in which opposing experts are lined up against one another and given equal airtime. While this seems equitable, the effect is to make it seem as though climate change 'believer' scientists are matched by an equal body of sceptics, when actually they vastly outnumber them. In practice, there is a strong consensus that global warming is a reality, that it is caused by human activities, that it will get worse and that action must be taken to prepare for the consequences.

Will we be able to tackle climate change?

The broad consensus among climate scientists is that the world must act to limit warming to a rise of 2°C at most, and that to do this will require CO_2 levels to be stabilised at around 450 parts per million, which means emissions must be reduced by at least 60 per cent of 1990 levels by 2050 (although a recent study suggests that even this would only give a 50 per cent chance of success). What is the world doing to achieve this?

The Kyoto Protocol
The primary effort to curb emissions and tackle climate change is the Kyoto Protocol, an international agreement signed in Kyoto in Japan in 1997, which sets targets for

industrialised nations to reduce their greenhouse gas emissions. Under the Protocol, which came into force on 16 February 2005, the industrialised countries that signed up have agreed to reduce their combined emissions by 5 per cent of 1990 levels by 2008–2010. Obviously this is a long way short of the 60 per cent mooted by climate scientists, but it would be a start.

Until the Russians somewhat unexpectedly signed up to the Kyoto Protocol in 2004 it looked like the agreement would not even be ratified and thus come into force as a binding international treaty. Despite this, however, Kyoto has inspired mixed feelings even among environmentalists, many of whom argue that it was fatally hamstrung before it even started. The most obvious drawback is that the world's biggest polluter, the US, is not a signatory (despite having been instrumental in drawing up the treaty), and neither are other major polluters such as Australia. Less developed nations – such as China, India and Brazil – are signed up to Kyoto, but under its terms they are not obligated to make any cuts in emissions, despite the fact that they are projected to be major emitters in the near future.

The tortured negotiation process also threw up various other revisions that some feel have undermined the treaty. Former US Presidential advisor and Yale University economist William Nordhaus has estimated that the impact of the US withdrawal and other revisions would be to slash the actual reduction achieved by Kyoto to just 1.5 per cent of a no-control scenario, assuming that the signatories did in fact meet their targets. Unfortunately the UN says that they are now well off target, and predicts that by 2010 emissions will actually be 10 per cent higher than in 1990.

Carbon trading

One substantive achievement of Kyoto was to institute the first carbon trading scheme, in the EU's Emissions Trading Scheme (EU ETS), which started up in January 2005. Carbon trading is a way to put an actual monetary value on the environmental cost of carbon emissions, which businesses normally do not pay for (see 'Poisoning the planet', Chapter 3). Like the rest of Kyoto, however, the EU ETS seems flawed from the off. Four EU countries have been left out altogether, and the EU has sued Italy and rowed with the UK over technical details. The way the scheme was structured means that it covers just half of carbon dioxide emissions produced in the EU, and other greenhouse gases (such as methane) are not included at all. The real test of the scheme's success is the value at which carbon ends up being traded. Experts calculate that in monetary terms the true cost to the environment of a tonne of carbon dioxide is about 20 euros. At present it is being traded at around 8 euros per tonne, which effectively means that the environment is still paying for business to pollute.

Alternative energy

Economic growth and reaching/maintaining developed world lifestyles depend on being able to supply ever greater amounts of energy. The only way to achieve this without increasing emissions is through non-fossil fuel energy production, which is therefore attractive to governments and businesses as well as environmentalists. However, there are fierce disputes about the economics and environmental impacts of most of the available alternative energy sources.

The problems of wind power amply illustrate those of the field of renewable energy as a whole. Generating electricity from wind through the use of turbines appears to be an extremely environmentally friendly option. But turbines are large and highly conspicuous, and considered to be an eyesore by many. The best locations for wind farms are often beauty spots or previously unspoiled landscapes/conservation areas. The turbines themselves need extensive anchors, so that installing them damages the local environment, while they need to be served by power lines that either disfigure the landscape with pylons or damage the terrain by being buried.

The economics of wind power are also suspect. The best spots for generation are usually very distant from consumers, which means long transmission distances with concomitant expense and inefficiency. Because wind is inconstant, wind power is not always on stream, so capacity needs to vastly outstrip possible demand. In Germany, for instance, by far the world's biggest wind power generator, wind farms make up 15 per cent of capacity but only produce 3 per cent of power. All this adds up to make wind power an extremely expensive form of electricity generation, which requires massive government subsidies to be viable. In a recent report, Germany's own Energy Agency concluded that investing in wind power was an inefficient use of limited resources that could produce more environmental benefit elsewhere.

Similar issues of environmental impact, distance between production and consumption, and question marks over technology and cost bedevil other forms of non-fossil fuel energy, such as biofuels, nuclear, tidal, geothermal, solar and hydroelectric power. None of them is sufficiently attractive in terms of price to offer a serious alternative to fossil fuels in the eyes of businesses and governments with an eye on the bottom line; at least not while the price of fossil fuels continues to fail to reflect their environmental costs.

Carbon sequestration

Sequestering (locking away) carbon after it has been emitted would avoid the need to curb emissions in the first place. Three main sequestration methods have been suggested, but all are problematic. Planting extensive forests to soak up carbon is already widely practised – when linked to wood-burning power stations, such a scheme allows carbon-neutral power generation. But as detailed above, warming may convert the forests into net carbon contributors. Pumping CO_2 underground is still in its technological infancy, and could be prohibitively expensive. Pouring fertiliser into the ocean to seed algal blooms, which then die and sink to the ocean floor, locking away carbon, raises obvious environmental issues. We know that such blooms are already damaging marine ecosystems; would it be wise to experiment with the ocean to try to sort out the mess we've made of the atmosphere?

Should we accept the inevitable?

It is evident that all of the strategies for limiting or soaking up emissions that are listed above are either costly or problematic or both. Some sceptics argue that money spent trying to curb emissions is wasted because climate change is not caused by human activities. Others are asking whether we should simply acknowledge that it is going to happen and focus resources on adapting to it, rather than trying vainly to beat back the tide. Leading environmental sceptic Dr Bjorn Lomborg recently told the BBC: 'There are actually many other things where we can do an enormous amount of good for fairly little money [eg tackling diseases or alleviating poverty], whereas Kyoto and other gains like that are going to be somewhere where we can do fairly little good at a very high cost.' This view argues that expensive environmental measures may or may not produce benefits at some point decades in the future, whereas there is a multitude of pressing problems facing the world today.

There is certainly a case to be made that alleviating poverty is more important than pursuing deferred environmental benefits. Firstly, on moral grounds, and secondly because rich societies generally cope better with environmental changes and problems than poorer ones. Surely, therefore, the prospects for coping with environmental change and dealing with its causes would be best served by making poor countries richer as quickly as possible?

However, there are major flaws in this argument. Environmental damage, and climate change in particular, are major causes of poverty. In a 2004 report, the Working Group on Climate Change and Development (a coalition of major development charities and environmental groups) warns that warming threatens the UN Millennium Development Goal of halving world poverty and could 'even reverse human development achievements', while the IPCC warns, 'The impacts of climate change will fall disproportionately upon developing countries and the poor …'

Another flaw is that the longer the world waits to act on climate change, the more expensive it will be. According to a study by Steffen Kallbekken of the Center for International Climate and Environmental Research in Oslo, Norway, a 20-year delay in curbing emissions will increase the size of necessary emissions curbs by three to seven times, with concomitantly greater pain for national economies. On balance, it seems that the sceptics are wrong, and that it is a good idea to try to curb emissions sooner rather than later. Arguing otherwise sounds suspiciously like an excuse to avoid making hard choices and a justification for continuing to live unsustainably by passing on the bill to later generations.

Reasons to be cheerful

A number of serious, well-costed studies suggest that curbing emissions sufficiently is not only possible, but might not even be ruinously expensive. For instance, an analysis by Professor John Schellnhuber, of the University of East Anglia, concludes that climate change could be brought under control for as little as 0.3 per cent of global gross domestic product. Experts say that there is no 'magic bullet' for successful emissions control, but that by adopting a mix or 'portfolio' of strategies, from energy efficiency and alternative energy to carbon trading and sequestration, large cuts can be achieved.

Reasons for pessimism

Unfortunately the reality of the situation on the ground offers grounds for serious gloom. The world's major current and future polluters are not part of the Kyoto effort, and under its current administration the US – the single largest carbon emitter with a quarter of worldwide emissions – resolutely opposes concerted international action on curbs and even questions whether climate change is really happening. Even governments that seem serious about tackling climate change are failing to live up to their commitments. Only four of the Kyoto signatories are on track to meet their targets, and even the UK, which is one of them, has recently attempted to make concessions to corporate polluters and is currently increasing its CO_2 emissions.

In fact, far from being curbed, emissions from many sectors are accelerating. In the UK, for instance, emissions from houses have risen by 11 per cent since 1990, despite the government's commitments to reduce emissions. To reverse this trend would require demolishing and replacing 14 per cent of UK homes. Is this likely to happen? Perhaps the most worrying statistic is for projected global energy demand over the next 25 years. According to the International Energy Agency's World Energy Outlook for 2004, world electricity demand is projected to double, and emissions of carbon dioxide from all sectors (including electricity) are likely to increase by 62 per cent. In the face of facts such as these, it seems unlikely that there is any realistic chance of curbing emissions by the 60 per cent necessary.

Too little, too late?

There seems to be a gulf between what the world needs to do and what it is doing/is likely to do. Climate science tells us that global systems have great inertia, and that there is a considerable time lag between inputs and effects. For instance, carbon dioxide released into the atmosphere remains for decades or even centuries, while it takes up to a thousand years for water that sank in the Arctic to resurface in the Tropics. Similarly, though on a shorter time scale, there is a time-lag effect in human systems. A power plant commissioned today, for instance, will have a lifespan of fifty years. The new Airbus A380, the world's largest passenger plane, is expected to set the air travel paradigm (and thus levels of emissions) for the next 30 years or more. So the course of climate change over the next few decades, and perhaps a lot longer, may already be determined. What's more, we may have already set in train processes that will awaken one of the 'sleeping giants' of climate change, in which case any response we make to climate change will be too little, too late.

Likelihood: 8
Damage: 6
Fear factor: 7

Waking the giants

It could already be too late to stop global warming; the planet may be irrevocably doomed to suffer runaway warming on a scale not seen for tens of millions of years. This worst-case global warming scenario will not be caused by human activities, such as industrial emissions – at least, not directly. Instead, it will result from the rousing of the 'sleeping giants' of the climate system.

The sleeping giants are factors that have the potential to alter global climate and sea levels irreversibly, and possibly very quickly. Normally they are not involved in the global climate system for one reason or another (hence 'sleeping'), but if conditions change beyond a certain threshold value they will become mobilised, setting in train processes that cannot be stopped. The main sleeping giants that could threaten to unleash irreversible climate change are: the Antarctic and Greenland ice caps; the methane sediments stored on land and under the oceans; and the biosphere's carbon cycle.

The Greenland ice cap

Very large quantities of water are locked up in the 2-kilometre thick ice cap that sits on Greenland. If this starts to melt, it could prove to be an irreversible, runaway process, since as the ice cap melts it thins and its upper surface drops in altitude.

Air at lower altitudes is warmer, so this would increase the rate of melting.

The Antarctic ice sheets

Huge quantities of water are also locked up in the ice sheets that sit on Antarctica. Normally these ice sheets hold back glaciers on the continent and restrict the rate at which they can flow into the sea. If there is a widespread break-up of Antarctic ice sheets, major glaciers could start to feed into the ocean, raising sea level simply by displacement.

Methane release

As a greenhouse gas, methane is 21 times more potent than carbon dioxide. Vast quantities – up to 5,000 billion tonnes – are stored in ocean sediments or locked away in permafrost on land. The deep ocean sediments are particularly vulnerable to warming, since they are stored in the form of frozen gas hydrates. Low temperatures and high pressure keep the methane in this form, but penetration of surface warming to the deep ocean could mobilise the frozen hydrates. This could turn into a runaway process – as initial hydrates expand into gas and bubble up to the surface, so the expansion causes an explosive depressurisation of the rest of the hydrates.

Warming on land is also likely to melt permafrozen soil and release terrestrial methane stores. There is even evidence that very minor temperature rises in tundra soils may be enough to revive dormant microbes, which in turn will begin to produce CO_2 and methane despite the ground remaining well below freezing point.

Biosphere effects

The biosphere is responsible for sequestering, or locking away, huge quantities of carbon. Carbon is taken in by plants and by animals that make carbonate skeletons (eg coral and plankton), and although much is released when they die, a lot is locked away in sediments that will eventually form new rocks. For instance, a significant proportion of the carbon in the atmosphere is sequestered by a species of phytoplankton called *Emiliania huxleyi,* which absorbs CO_2 to form tiny plates of calcium carbonate. When the phytoplankton dies, these plates rain down to the sea bottom and become sediments. The quantities of carbon involved dwarf the amounts of carbon emitted by human activities. This means that if we inadvertently alter the global carbon cycle by interfering with the biosphere, in particular the ocean ecosystem, we could indirectly cause a massive change in levels of atmospheric carbon dioxide.

One way in which this could happen is ocean acidification, itself the result of human activities pumping CO_2 into the atmosphere where it is absorbed by the ocean (see Chapter 3). Acidification interferes with calcification – the formation of calcium carbonate skeletons by marine organisms.

What will happen if the giants awake?

Computer models, together with evidence from the past, show that once the Greenland ice cap starts to melt it cannot be stopped without a new global Ice Age. It contains enough water to raise sea levels by 7 metres, but this pales in comparison to the Antarctic ice sheets. If the western Antarctic ice sheet breaks up and Antarctic glaciers flow into the ocean unchecked, the resulting rise in sea levels could be great enough to float the eastern ice sheet and increase the danger of it breaking up. Then we would really be in trouble: the eastern sheet contains enough water to raise global sea levels by 50 metres. As with the Greenland ice cap, once begun this process could only be reversed when the planet slips into a new Ice Age.

Methane poses a double threat. Its extreme greenhouse potency means that release of massive quantities from ocean and/or permafrost sediments would trigger accelerated global warming that would be impossible for humans to reverse. Methane also reacts with oxygen in the atmosphere to produce carbon dioxide – if enough is released, atmospheric oxygen levels may drop too low to support animal life, and we would simply suffocate.

If the ocean becomes too acidic, calcification will slow or stop, and CO_2 that would normally be removed will be left in the atmosphere. Without *Emiliania huxleyi* and its ilk, we could be looking at a runaway greenhouse effect that would boost temperatures by 10°C or more.

Between them, these sleeping giants have the potential to destroy civilisation. A temperature increase of 10°C or more, together with massive sea level rises, would drastically undermine global agriculture, swamp most of the populated areas of Earth and lead to mass extinctions and catastrophic changes in the global ecosystem. Mankind has survived such major climate swings before, but civilisations have not.

Has it happened before?

The geological record suggests that these sleeping giants have indeed been roused in the past, with dramatic consequences for global climate. At several times the polar ice caps have melted completely, raising sea levels massively. Some of these warming events may have been linked to massive methane releases, which are thought to have helped to end Ice Ages, and may even have been responsible for a mass extinction event 251 million years ago. Some palaeontologists think that a huge methane release at the end of the Permian era may have reduced atmospheric oxygen levels from 35 to 12 per cent over 20,000 years, literally suffocating up to 90 per cent of land animals and radically altering marine ecosystems as well. Another great wave of extinctions saw the end of the dinosaurs, together with a massive die-off of marine life that disrupted the ocean ecosystem. This may have been linked to a rise in atmospheric CO_2 levels at the time, as the main driver of the global carbon cycle was interrupted.

How likely is it to happen?

There is a lot of speculation in the science surrounding these sleeping giants, and many climate scientists dismiss the warnings as unnecessarily alarmist. Unfortunately, however, there is evidence that some of the giants may be stirring. In the Antarctic, for instance, rising temperatures already seem to be causing break up of the western Antarctic ice sheet (which is particularly vulnerable because it largely rests on water) and major western glaciers are flowing faster as a result. Meanwhile in Greenland there is evidence that the ice cap is melting fast. According to *New Scientist* magazine, the tipping point for irreversible melting of the Greenland ice cap is a temperature rise of 2.7°C, which is well within many of the estimates for warming by 2100.

Methane release is known to occur from sediments in the Arctic during the summer months, which shows that rising temperatures do have an effect on methane sediments beneath the ocean. Whether there is an immediate threat is less clear – some models suggest we won't have to worry for a while.

Ocean acidification is already underway, but no one really knows how severe the impact on the ocean ecosystem will be. For instance, *Emiliania huxleyi* has not always been the dominant carbonate-forming phytoplankton species in the ocean; at other times, other species filled the role of moving carbon from the atmosphere to the sea bottom. So even if acidification kills off *Emiliania huxleyi*, another species could take over, unless, as some scientists fear, the acidification happens too fast and other species cannot adapt in time.

The uncertainty surrounding the sleeping giants does not mean they should be taken lightly. Most scientists agree that there is still time to take action to limit global warming so that the giants are not stirred from their slumber. If we ignore the warnings, however, we will set in motion irreversible changes.

Likelihood: 3
Damage: 9
Fear factor: 4

A new Ice Age

Until the threat of global warming reared its head in the 1970s and 80s, the climate doomsday that was most feared was a new Ice Age: a plunge in temperatures that would see much of the Northern Hemisphere covered in ice or frozen tundra. This threat seems to have receded with the advent of global warming, but the intricate mechanism of the Earth's climate means that, paradoxically, warming could actually trigger a new Ice Age. How is this possible?

Steady states and tipping points

Research into past climates indicates that most of the time negative feedback loops maintain the climate in a relatively steady state, damping down fluctuations (such as those caused by volcanoes pumping gas into the atmosphere) to keep average temperatures within a narrow range. However, if the fluctuations exceed a certain threshold the global climate reaches a tipping point and positive feedback cycles swing into action, causing a rapid switch to a different climatic steady state. This tipping process can cause average temperatures to plunge by as much as 8°C in just two decades, a considerable difference considering that the last Ice Age was only 4 or 5°C colder than today. But what could cause warming to tip the climate into a new Ice Age?

Gulf Stream shutdown

Northwest Europe is at roughly the same latitude as Newfoundland and Siberia, but enjoys much higher average temperatures and a temperate climate. This is because the ocean current called the Gulf Stream flows past its shores, transferring heat from the tropical regions. It is part of the ocean's thermohaline circulation – currents driven by differences in temperature and salinity.

How does the Stream work?

The Gulf Stream is a surface current that is drawn past Europe by a thermohaline 'pump' off the coast of Greenland. As water in the Arctic Ocean freezes into ice it leaves behind dense, salty water that sinks, flowing back down to the Equator along the ocean floor and drawing in more water behind it at surface levels (the Gulf Stream).

Shutting down the pump

If the water off the Greenland coast becomes less salty and/or warmer it will no longer be dense enough to sink and the pump will be turned off. The Gulf Stream will cease to flow and Northwest Europe will be plunged into a climatic regime akin to that of Newfoundland.

The shutdown of the pump could be triggered by global warming in a number of ways. Warming could reduce ice formation and give warmer, less dense water. It could also cause more ice to melt and increase rainfall, boosting freshwater discharge from Artic meltwater and Arctic rivers and thus decreasing the salinity of the water, again making it less dense.

What will happen if there is a new Ice Age?

The short-term effects of shutdown of the Gulf Stream would be to bring much colder weather to Northwestern Europe, more than counteracting the effects of global warming, while

Alaska would heat up even more rapidly and the Asian monsoon might fail (causing massive famine). The longer-term outcomes are highly uncertain. Either the local cooling will be only a blip in an otherwise steady heating trend, or it could be the trigger that causes the delicately balanced global climate-determining systems to flip over into a rapid cooling state, ushering in a new Ice Age.

On the evidence of previous Ice Ages, this would result in vast ice sheets kilometres thick advancing southwards to cover North America, Europe and Asia as far as New York, London and Moscow, while the lands ahead of the ice would be reduced to frozen tundra blasted by howling winds and bitter frosts. South of the tundra, there would be regions of pine forest and grass steppe, also subject to bitterly cold winters with only the briefest of summers. Although the Southern Hemisphere would experience much less glaciation, the world as a whole would become cooler and drier, causing rainforests to shrink and deserts to spread. Sea levels would drop dramatically, exposing huge areas of continental shelf, making many sea routes impassable but opening up land bridges between continents and islands. This would allow some species to spread at the expense of others, diminishing biodiversity already depleted by the climate changes.

How civilisation would fare amongst all this would depend on the rate of cooling. If past climate changes are anything to go by, this could be very fast. Some scientists believe the Gulf Stream could shut down almost overnight, while a global temperature plunge could take as little as twenty years. Civilisation would not be able to cope with this. Agriculture would fail, infrastructure would be destroyed and society would no longer be able to feed or warm itself.

Has it happened before?

Proxy sources, such as sediment cores from the ocean bottom, show that the Gulf Stream has shut down repeatedly in the past, and suggest that while the shutdown could happen in just a few days, it could take millennia to turn back on. Ice Ages in general have characterised the last few hundred thousand years of Earth's history. They have been interspersed with shorter warm periods called interglacials. Civilisation has arisen in the interglacial since the last Ice Age, so there is no way of knowing how it would respond to a new one.

The closest parallel that history offers is a period known as the Little Ice Age, which lasted from around 1500 to 1850 CE. During this time average Northern Hemisphere temperatures were around 0.4°C lower than the late 20th century average. This does not sound like much, but among the results were frost fairs on the frozen River Thames, pack ice seen off the coast of England, and serious consequences for European societies. For instance, the Little Ice Age caused the collapse of Norse society in Greenland, drove European fishing fleets across the Atlantic, and helped to inspire the Agricultural Revolution of the 18th century and the colonisation of North America. Civilisation did not fail, but societies were certainly changed. How much greater might be the impact of a drop in temperatures of 4 or 5°C or more?

How likely is it to happen?

Disturbingly there is evidence that the conditions for shutting down the thermohaline pump that drives the Gulf Current are already being met. Arctic rivers are discharging more freshwater, major Greenland glaciers are flowing faster and Arctic ice is melting. Measurements suggest that deep ocean currents flowing southwards in the North Atlantic have slowed by 20 per cent over the last 50 years and that biodiversity in the North Atlantic may be changing to reflect a weakening of the thermohaline circulation.

Playing with ice

In his book *A Guide to the End of the World*, Professor Bill McGuire points out that a temperature profile spanning the last 15,000 years appears to show that we are nearing the end of an interglacial (a period of high temperatures between Ice Ages, characterised by a rapid initial rise in temperature and a slow but accelerating cooling trend thereafter). Recent centuries have bucked this trend, probably because of warming caused by human activities, but the overall temperature profile closely resembles that of the previous interglacial, which led to the last Ice Age. McGuire warns that the tail end of an interglacial is a dangerous time to be experimenting with the climate, because global climate systems are poised on a knife-edge between the two major steady states. Through its effect on major systems like the thermohaline circulation, warming caused by human activities could be the trigger that tips climate from a warm state to an icy one.

Likelihood: 3
Damage: 8
Fear factor: 3

Conclusion: Prepare for the worst

Global warming is almost certainly under way, and the chances of preventing a rise of 2°C or more by the end of the century look very slim. Of itself, such a rise would bring higher sea levels, wild weather and frequent natural disasters, and threaten food security, infrastructure and the global economy. The poor would be worst affected, and while living standards would probably be diminished for everyone, warming would increase global inequality, with knock-on effects such as war, terrorism and mass migration. Civilisation would survive, but in straitened circumstances that would threaten many of our fundamental values and aspirations.

Chapter 5
Cataclysm

The people of New Zealand emerged, blinking, from the shelters and bunkers to which they had retreated three days earlier. A steady rain of light ash fell from the sky; a horrible roiling mass of thick grey clouds shot through with sickly yellow streaks. Weak light filtered through the overcast to reveal the blackened, burnt-over remains of their cities and countryside. A few patches of vegetation seemed almost untouched, but in built-up areas the rain of molten debris had quickly set off firestorms that had raised whole cities. Surveying the ruins, the people breathed a sigh of relief. They had got off lightly.

Everyone knew his or her role in the aftermath, at least as well as six months of training and preparation allowed. They gathered at their staging posts, gratefully received the first round of rations and waited for news of the rest of the planet. It was not good; though Australia, South East Asia and parts of China and Japan were able to respond, there was only silence from North and South America, Africa, Western Asia and Europe. It took three weeks for the first reconnaissance missions to bring back word, and when it was announced, it was far worse than even the most pessimistic had dreamed. The impact, the blastwave, the firestorm, the tsunamis and the rain of ejecta had vaporised much of Europe and Africa, scoured clean much of the Americas and ignited the rest of the planet, and from the giant scar in the Earth's surface there now poured forth a torrent of molten lava, accompanied by vast plumes of choking sulphur and other noxious gases.

The New Zealanders realised just how bad this was when they received the next round of rations – they had been halved. The authorities knew that the outlook for the planet was much more bleak than predicted. Since the initial fires had cooled the temperature had dropped sharply. In the permanent gloom the emergency farms had simply failed. The stockpiled reserves were running low; there was no way to replenish them. The land was barren, the sea little more than a dirty slurry of acid, wet ash and rotting biomass.

Four weeks later, the first food rioting began. A crowd of angry labourers had gathered round a distribution centre demanding supplements and extra clothing for their children, who were suffering from rickets, frostbite and hypothermia. But there were no supplements to be had, no clothes and no more food. Over the next two months, the emergency government in Wellington lost touch with outlying districts as law and order broke down. By the fourth month after the impact, the main bunker in Wellington was an armed fortress, beating off suicide attacks from desperate mobs of starving people. The government had long since lost contact with other nations, and their pleas for help had not been answered. The remaining fuel and food rations were given to the elite Pathfinder crew, and the last serviceable plane was readied for a final, futile search for help. The prime minister didn't waste his strength going to watch it take off. In the vault at the bottom of the main bunker, he slowly assembled the materials he had prepared a few months earlier when it became obvious this outcome was inevitable. The time capsule complete, he uttered a silent prayer and sealed the giant doors. Some record, at least, would survive.

Extinction level events

The other chapters in this book describe scenarios that could destroy civilisation, but few seriously threaten the survival of our species. In this chapter, however, you will discover several ways in which humanity could be destroyed altogether, and you will learn that this outcome is not merely possible, but highly probable. Mankind has survived many rigours in the course of its million years or so of evolution, from dramatic climate swings to enormous eruptions, but it has never had to deal with an extinction level event (ELE) – a cataclysmic geological or astronomical event that is so destructive it results in mass extinctions. Life on Earth has survived around 25 of these, but arguably the reason we are here today, instead of dinosaurs or trilobites, is because life held on only by the skin of its teeth. Given enough time, it is almost certain that another ELE will threaten the Earth, while even relatively minor versions of them could doom, or at least dent, civilisation. This chapter describes ELE candidates both serious and far-fetched, from comet and asteroid impacts, massive volcanic eruptions and mega-tsunamis, to gamma-ray bursts, wandering black holes and pole reversals.

Comet and asteroid impacts

The Solar System began life as a disc of gas, dust and chunks of rock and ice. When the first planets coalesced out of the chaos, they swept up much of the material, clearing great swathes of the disc. Over the next 2 billion years much of the rest of the rock and ice rained down on the young planets, subjecting them to a constant bombardment. Eventually the Solar System cleared to the point where large chunks of rock or ice became quite rare, and were mostly confined to a couple of belts in the middle and the far fringes of the system. There remain, nonetheless, millions of asteroids (space rocks) and an unknown number of comets (giant chunks of ice, rock and dust) orbiting the Sun. Many of these follow an orbit that crosses that of the Earth, so that there is a chance they might collide with it. Such impacts happen hundreds of times a day, but almost always involve small asteroids, which burn up in the Earth's atmosphere and never reach the surface. Occasionally, however, a big asteroid, or even a comet, crosses path with our planet, smashing into it with terrible force and causing death and destruction on a planetary scale. Until recently, it was not appreciated that this could happen to Earth, or that it actually does happen with alarming regularity. We now know that, over a long time scale, your chances of dying because of an impact are roughly equivalent to your chances of dying in an air crash.

What will happen if an asteroid or comet hits the Earth?

The damage caused depends on the size and speed of the body. An asteroid 50 metres across is big enough to destroy a city. An asteroid 500 metres across could devastate an entire country. An asteroid 1 kilometre or more in diameter threatens to cause global destruction and produce serious climate change, while a truly huge asteroid 10 kilometres or more in diameter would cause an ELE. This was the size of the asteroid that caused the Chicxulub impact, which is thought to have helped wipe out the dinosaurs, 65 million years ago. Comets can be 100 kilometres or more in diameter, and travel three times faster than most asteroids, giving them more energy. A cometary impact would also result in an ELE.

The big one

What will happen to the planet if a 10 kilometre-wide Chicxulub-style asteroid hits us? The impact would leave a crater 180 kilometres wide, blasting through to the deepest layers of the Earth's crust and triggering earthquakes around the planet. A huge fireball, hotter than the Sun, would bloom and the blast wave would flatten an entire continent. The heat and force of the impact would generate enormous winds or hypercanes (cyclones that are five times more powerful than the worst hurricanes) across the whole planet. If the initial impact was in the ocean, gigantic tsunamis, 150 metres high or more, would spread out and scour all the lands around the ocean rim, racing 300 kilometres inland. Huge quantities of rock, known as ejecta, would be flung up from the impact, some of it into space. As it fell back to Earth the heat of re-entry would generate a rain of fire, triggering immense wildfires all round the globe. Up to a quarter of all terrestrial biomass would be reduced to ash.

Huge quantities of dust from the impact, ash and smoke from the fires, and water and salt from the ocean would be blasted high into the stratosphere, along with many noxious gases generated by the heat of the initial fireball and the subsequent firestorm. Soon the entire planet would be screened off from sunlight, possibly for years to come, causing what astronomer Victor Clube calls a 'cosmic winter'. Temperatures would plummet by up to 15°C, and there would be too little light for any surviving plants to photosynthesise. Acid rain and toxic smoke would poison the oceans and kill up to

three-quarters of all marine life. When the cosmic winter finally cleared, the world would be subjected to what Andrew
Blaustein, a professor of zoology at Oregon State University,
calls a 'UV spring', as the ozone layer would have been destroyed
by the salt and noxious gases produced by the impact.

Another alarming possibility is that the impact might
punch a hole through the Earth's crust and unleash a flood of
lava. Recent research has suggested that several major extinction events – including the Chicxulub impact – apparently
coincided with huge lava floods, and some lava floods have
been directly linked to impacts. Lava floods can have catastrophic effects on the Earth's climate similar to those of an
impact (see 'Super-volcano', below).

In short, a 10 kilometre-wide asteroid would probably wipe
out a large proportion of life on Earth. Virtually all humans
would be killed – either almost immediately through the initial impact effects, or as a result of starvation and cold during
the subsequent cosmic winter. Some people might survive by
hiding in very deep bunkers equipped with enough supplies
to last for several years. Given the adaptability of the human
species, these few survivors might be able to negotiate the UV
spring and repopulate a slowly recovering world, but it would
not be certain. If the impact body was a giant comet – a monster 100 kilometres wide – it is hard to see how any life on
Earth could survive, except for microbes in deep strata and
the occasional scavenging organism on the surface.

City-killers and country-devastators

Even smaller impacts could change history and threaten civilisation. A 50 metre-wide asteroid that fell on a major city
could kill millions. If New York, Tokyo or London were to be

levelled like this, how would the global economy respond? A 500 metre-wide asteroid falling into the ocean could generate tsunamis big enough to wipe out every coastal city in a hemisphere, killing 500 million people or more. An asteroid 1 kilometre in diameter – generally considered to be the threshold for a serious threat to civilisation – would generate impact energy of 100,000 megatons, leaving a 20 kilometre-wide crater and instantly vaporising a zone 500 kilometres in diameter. Depending on where it fell, it could easily kill tens of millions of people directly, and many more through tsunamis, falling ejecta and fires. The debris blasted into the atmosphere could bring on a year-long cosmic winter. According to some estimates, up to half of the global population would die in the resulting famine.

Has it happened before?

A chunk of rock that reaches the surface of the Earth is known as a meteorite. There seem to be few if any confirmed deaths from meteorite impact in the whole of recorded history, which is incredible given the number of large rocks that have crashed to Earth over the last few thousand years. But there is plenty of evidence of major impacts both recently and in geological history. 'City-killer'-size meteors have hit the Earth three times in the past century, but always in remote places, and apparently without loss of life. The most recent case was an impact in Greenland, in 1997.

The Earth bears the scars of much greater impacts. There are 165 known impact craters on the planet. Of the 25 massive extinctions known from the fossil records, 7 of them have been linked to impacts. The best known is the Chicxulub impact event, 65 million year ago, which marked the end of the Cretaceous era and is thought to have helped wipe out two-thirds of all species, including the dinosaurs.

But this was not the last time that a potential ELE-size impact occurred. Recent satellite mapping of Antarctica suggests that a 10 kilometre-wide asteroid ploughed into the planet 780,000 years ago, but fortunately for the early humans living in Africa at the time the impact was a long way off and coincided with an Ice Age. The thick ice sheets probably helped to dampen the effects (eg weakening the tsunami and reducing the amount of ejecta), so that this impact did not cause an ELE and early man survived.

The worst mass extinction in Earth's history, known as the Permo-Triassic extinction, has also recently been linked to an impact. Researchers claim to have detected a crater in deep strata off the coast of Australia, and to have dated it to 250 million years ago – the time of the Permo-Triassic extinction that wiped out 70 per cent of terrestrial life and 95 per cent of marine life.

But perhaps the most terrifying impact in history was on another planet. In 1993 fragments of the comet Shoemaker-Levy crashed into Jupiter, watched by many of Earth's astronomers. The largest fragment left an impact scar wider than the Earth. It was this event that first alerted public opinion and world governments to the severity of the threat from outer space – proving that there were objects in the Solar System that could virtually destroy the planet.

How likely is it to happen?

The chances of a major impact depend on how many objects there are in space with an orbit that might cross that of the

Earth. Astronomers can detect many of the asteroids near the Earth, and have produced estimates of the numbers of Earth Crossing Asteroids (ECAs). It is estimated that there are 100,000 ECAs 100 metres+ in diameter, 20,000 ECAs 500 metres+ and, according to NASA's Jet Propulsion Lab, there are between 500 and 1,000 ECAs bigger than 1 kilometre in diameter. More than 300 of these have been observed and are known not to pose a danger for at least several hundred years. In fact, out of all the known ECAs only 13 are believed to have any chance of crossing our orbit before 2100.

More dangerous than these known asteroids are objects that haven't been spotted yet. Most dangerous of all are comets, which are basically invisible until they reach the inner Solar System and develop a tail. By the time Earth-astronomers spot a comet that is headed towards us, it could be less than six months away.

Even if we don't know for sure what's out there, we can estimate the average probabilities of impacts of different magnitudes if we know how often they have happened in the past. However, there are differing views on the frequency with which impacts occur. Some experts argue for a uniformitarian view, which holds that the frequency of impacts is relatively constant over time, so that our current risk of being hit is the same as the risk for the last few hundred million years. Other experts espouse a theory called coherent catastrophism, which maintains that impacts become more frequent at some points in time.

Uniformitarian frequency

If the uniformitarians are correct, and impacts happen at a constant rate, we can say that a 50-metre asteroid, big enough to level a city, hits the Earth on average once or twice a century. Fortunately the size of the Earth means that many of these will fall onto wilderness areas, although an ocean impact would generate killer tsunamis.

A 500-metre asteroid, big enough to devastate a country, hits the Earth every 10,000 years, on average. A 1-kilometre asteroid, big enough to threaten civilisation, can be expected every 100,000–333,000 years, while an ELE would only be expected every 50–100 million years. It is important to understand that these numbers do not mean that a 500-metre asteroid, for instance, lands regularly every 10,000 years, and that we can count from the last one that landed to work out when the next one will impact. What the numbers refer to is the probability of an impact of this magnitude. If the probability that a 500-metre asteroid will hit the Earth this year is 10,000 to 1, it means that over a period of 10,000 years you would expect one such impact to happen.

To help quantify the true risk posed by a Near-Earth Object (NEO), Richard Binzel of MIT devised the Torino scale, which takes into account both the probability of an impact and the scale of damage that it would cause. A Torino score of 0 means that either an impact has virtually no chance of happening, or that it will not cause any significant damage. A Torino score of 10 refers to an impact that is 100 per cent certain to happen, and that will devastate life on Earth. So far there are no known space objects that merit a Torino score higher than 0, and Binzel says that the chances of an object that rates a 10 coming along during the next century are less than 1 in 1,000.

Coherent Catastrophism

Many of the above estimates could be wrong, however, if the coherent catastrophists are right, and the frequency of impacts is not constant. There are two main theories about why this should be: one centres on the 'Oort Cloud', and the other around the 'Taurid Complex'.

The Oort Cloud theory

Astronomers believe that beyond the orbit of Pluto, in the outer reaches of the Solar System, is a ring of comet-like debris known as the Oort Cloud. Here lies much of the debris left over from the formation of the Solar System, including icy chunks of all sizes. Occasionally one of these chunks is somehow knocked out of its orbit and adopts an elliptical or parabolic orbit that eventually causes it to swing into the inner Solar System, where it becomes a comet (this is due to the Sun's solar wind – the stream of particles it gives off – knocking tiny fragments of ice from the chunk so that it develops a tail and becomes visible).

According to some theories of coherent catastrophism, the Oort Cloud periodically experiences large-scale perturbations (gravitational disturbances) that knock large numbers of chunks into eccentric orbits and thus trigger a shower of closely grouped comets. When this train of comets swings into the inner Solar System and crosses the orbit of the Earth, the chances of a collision are radically increased.

But what causes these gravitational disturbances in the Oort Cloud? Perhaps an unknown tenth planet, known as Planet X, orbits far beyond Pluto, or maybe even a dark companion to our own Sun – the type of 'dead' star known as a Brown Dwarf. One theory, the 'Shiva hypothesis', is that the perturbation is caused by the gravitational influence of the bulge in the centre of our galaxy. This theory is based on the fact that the Solar System orbits the galactic centre in an undulating pattern, so that every 26–30 million years it passes through the galactic plane. At this point the gravitational influence of the centre is particularly strong and knocks loose a string of comets from the Oort Cloud, some of which eventually smash into the Earth, so that it experiences ELEs roughly every 26–30 million years. The Solar System last passed through the galactic plane a few million years ago, which means that if a mass of comets were indeed knocked loose they should be hurtling towards us right now, invisible in the blackness of the outer Solar System but poised to flare into life when they are just six months away from planet Earth.

The Taurid theory

Another coherent catastrophist theory is based on the Taurid Complex. The Taurids are a meteor shower that lights up the night skies every winter as the Earth passes through the trail of debris left by an ancient comet, which broke up in the inner Solar System about 20,000 years ago. This debris trail mostly consists of small flecks and specks, which burn up harmlessly in the atmosphere to provide a light show, but there are also much larger chunks including Comet Encke (a periodic comet similar to Halley's Comet). These large chunks are grouped together and, according to the British astronomers Victor Clube and Bill Napier, the Earth passes through this part of the tail every 2,500–3,000 years, whereupon large numbers of impacts rock the planet. Supposedly this happened during the Bronze Age, around 2300 BCE, and the rain of fire from the heavens, and the resulting tsunamis, fires, famines and climate changes destroyed major civilisations in the Mediterranean and Near East, as well as bringing catastrophe to far-flung communities such as those at Skara Brae in the Orkneys. The theory says that the last time the Earth passed through the Taurid Complex the rain of cometary fragments helped to end the Roman Empire and usher in the Dark Ages in Europe.

The Taurid Complex theory is regarded with suspicion by most experts, not least because of the lack of evidence of actual impacts (eg craters), however there is some circumstantial evidence to back it up. If it is correct, then the next wave of impacts would not be expected until around 3200 CE.

Earth vs the asteroids

Whether the uniformitarians or the coherent catastrophists are correct, it is certain that at some point in the future another ELE-size object will menace the Earth with a 100 per cent chance of hitting us. Fortunately, however, the absence of a major impact for many thousands of years has allowed civilisation to advance to the point where we might be able to fend off doom. Successfully defending ourselves against space hazards means first being able to detect any threatening object, and second being able to destroy or deflect it.

Partly prompted by the Shoemaker-Levy collision with Jupiter, world governments and institutions set up a series of initiatives – such as the Spaceguard Foundation and the Spacewatch project – to look for NEOs that might be dangerous. The UK's Astrometry and Photometry Programme for NEOs, for instance, discovers 30–40 NEOs a month, and has so far logged more than 3,000. At least five other teams of scientists are also searching for dangerous NEOs, and should have assessed 90 per cent of the biggest ones within a decade.

Assuming, therefore, that an approaching object is spotted before it reaches us, what could be done about it? The Hollywood answer is to assemble some sort of super-nuke, or fleet of nuclear missiles, and simply blow it to smithereens, but most scientists think this would probably be a bad idea. Little is known about the composition or geology of asteroids and comets, so it is hard to predict how one would respond to a nuclear explosion. It is quite possible that this would simply create smaller rocks that would hit the Earth nonetheless. The preferred option would be to deflect the asteroid or comet. Even a tiny nudge could be enough to ensure that it misses the Earth, if applied early enough. Ideas for how to achieve this include firing lasers at the object, fitting rockets to it, using nuclear weapons or attaching a solar sail to it.

All of these lie, at present, in the realm of science fiction, but both NASA and the European Space Agency (ESA) either have or are planning missions to explore the options and gather data on geology. At the time of writing, NASA's Deep Impact mission is scheduled to rendezvous with Comet Tempel on 4 July 2005, when it will attempt to impact a small spacecraft into the comet and make extensive observations. Meanwhile the ESA are currently drawing up plans for the Don Quijote mission, which will attempt the same thing with a 500-metre asteroid.

Given enough time to develop missions like these, and more ambitious follow-up ones, it seems likely that we will learn how to deflect asteroids and even comets before they hit the Earth. But there are many uncertainties. A dangerous asteroid or comet might not be detected until the last moment, in which case there would be little or no time to launch a mission, even if we had the know-how. And there is the possibility that a truly enormous comet could come hurtling towards us – one too big for any human technology to deflect. Even a near-miss could have terrible consequences. A huge object passing within a few hundred miles of the Earth would produce enormous tidal forces that could in turn produce massive surges, swamping all of the planet's coastal zones – where the majority of the world's population now lives. On balance, however, given the relatively low odds of a 'doomsday'-size impact and the chances of developing protective technology, civilisation is probably not seriously threatened by an asteroid or comet impact.

Likelihood: 1
Damage: 10
Fear factor: 2

Super-volcano

Seventy-four thousand years ago mankind was almost wiped out by an enormous volcanic eruption that changed the global climate. A similar eruption could occur almost any day, with equally cataclysmic results. In fact a super-volcano is probably the greatest natural threat that humanity faces, and there is nothing we can do about it.

A super-volcanic eruption involves the explosive release of a vast reservoir of molten rock, or magma, to produce an eruption on a scale far beyond the experience of any living person. One of the best scales for measuring eruptions is the Volcanic Explosivity Index (VEI), which takes into account both the magnitude of the eruption – in other words, how much stuff is blown out of the Earth's crust – and the intensity of the eruption – how quickly it is blown out. The scale is logarithmic, so a VEI 5 eruption is ten times bigger than a VEI 4, and 100 times greater than a VEI 3. The two best-known eruptions of recent decades were the 1980 eruption of Mount St Helens, in the US, and the 1991 eruption of Mount Pinatubo, in the Philippines, which scored 5 and 6 respectively on the VEI scale. A super-volcano is one that scores a monstrous 8, making it 100 times more powerful than the Mount Pinatubo eruption and a staggering 1,000 times more powerful than the one at Mount St Helens.

What will happen if a super-volcano erupts?

A super-volcano will cause almost immediate total devastation in the region where it erupts, but over a longer period of time it will also affect the rest of the planet. The initial eruption could happen practically anywhere on the planet, but is thought to be particularly likely at the site of a previous super-volcano. These sites are known as calderas – giant depressions in the Earth's surface below which there may yet be a huge reservoir of magma. A major caldera that is often fingered as the most likely spot for a future super-eruption is at Yellowstone National Park in Wyoming.

If a super-volcano erupted at Yellowstone it would have an effect equivalent to the impact of a 1.5-kilometre diameter asteroid. The explosion would blast an 80 kilometre-wide hole in the Earth's crust, unleashing a devastating firestorm known as a pyroclastic flow. A pyroclastic flow is a hurricane of super-heated gas, molten globs of rock, and red-hot ash and dust. An area of 1,000 square kilometres would be obliterated in minutes. Ash from the eruption would blanket three quarters of the US to a depth of many centimetres. When lashing rain fell from storms generated by the volcano, much of this would become mud, generating killer mudslides that would swamp areas that had escaped the initial fallout.

Enormous quantities of gas and particles would be blasted into the atmosphere, including sulphur, chlorine, bromine and fluorine. At surface level this would cause choking, respiratory illness and poisoning, contaminating land where it fell for many years. But it would be in the upper atmosphere that the super-volcano would have its most harmful effects. The force of the eruption would blast sulphur and other particles into the stratosphere, and here they would combine with water vapour to generate thick clouds that would screen out a high proportion of the Sun's radiation. As much as 99 per cent of sunlight might be blocked, making the day as dark as night and stopping all photosynthesis. A volcanic winter lasting for years would follow. Temperatures would plummet by 5–10ºC, and possibly as much as 15ºC around the Tropics.

Most of the population of the local Yellowstone region would be killed almost immediately. Hundreds of thousands more across the Mid-West, West and Central US would be killed by ash, clouds of fumes and mud. But the real global death toll would result from the volcanic winter. If sunlight levels fell below the threshold for photosynthesis, almost all plant life on land and in the ocean would die (while the ocean would also become toxic as it soaked up the poisonous fumes from the eruption). Inevitably most of the rest of life on Earth would follow. Even developed nations do not maintain food reserves to last more than a couple of months, so rations would soon run out and society would fall apart as people struggled for sustenance and warmth. Few would survive a volcanic winter that lasted for several years. Admittedly this is a worst-case scenario. A volcanic winter might not cause such complete global dimming, and might last for 'only' a year, but even this would still cause global cooling and mass famine and its inevitable consequences.

Even after the volcanic winter had passed the danger would not be over. The chlorine and bromine emitted during a super-eruption would destroy much of the ozone layer that protects the Earth from UV radiation, so any surviving plants, animals or humans would have to contend with a 'UV spring' similar to that which might follow a nuclear or cosmic winter.

Flood basalts

An alternative form of super-volcano is a flood basalt event. Flood basalts are formed by an eruption which is not explosive, but which releases a massive flood of lava for a sustained period of time – centuries or more. Hundreds of thousands of cubic kilometres can pour out of the Earth's crust, covering up to a million square kilometres. At the same time, huge quantities of gas are released – including chlorine and bromine that destroy ozone, sulphur that causes both acid rain on a global scale and a period of global dimming, and enough carbon dioxide to generate a powerful greenhouse effect to follow the initial cooling. Flood basalt events are heavily implicated in major extinction events in the past, raising the possibility that a new event could threaten mankind in the future.

Has it happened before?

The biggest volcanic eruption since the last Ice Age was the eruption of Tambora, in Indonesia, in 1815. This was a VEI 7 event, which blew 50 cubic kilometres of ash into the atmosphere and caused global cooling of around 0.7°C, enough to cause the famous 'year without a summer' in 1816 and contribute to famine in many parts of the world. But Tambora was too small to be counted as a super-volcano.

The last true super-eruption was 73,500 years ago when Toba, in Northern Sumatra, exploded with devastating effects. Between 3,000 and 6,000 cubic kilometres of material was blasted into the atmosphere, and enough sulphur to create 5 billion tonnes of sulphur aerosol was thrown into the stratosphere. The amount of sunlight reaching the Earth may have been cut by 99 per cent, stopping global photosynthesis, while average global temperatures dropped by 5 or 6°C in just a few months – equivalent to a new Ice Age. The volcanic winter lasted for 6 years and may well have triggered the last Ice Age. DNA studies show that the human population experienced a 'bottleneck' at this time. Almost everyone alive was wiped out and for 20,000 years there were only a few thousand humans on the planet. Our species came perilously close to extinction, graphically illustrating the doomsday potential of a super-volcano.

The last flood basalt event was in the Columbia River area of the US, about 16 million years ago, but this was a relatively minor one. Much bigger ones include the Deccan Traps, in India, about 65 million years ago, and the Siberian Traps, about 250 million years ago. ('Trap' is a Sanskrit word meaning 'step', and describes the step-like appearance of the rock formations left by successive layers of lava flooding over the landscape.) Many palaeontologists do not think it is a coincidence that these are also the dates of major extinction events. The massive, sustained release of gases from the eruptions may have caused violent temperature swings from waves of global dimming and greenhouse warming, which in turn would have played havoc with the global ecosystem, wiping out all but a few species.

How likely is it to happen?

A super-eruption is thought to be 5 to 10 times more likely than an asteroid impact, and according to Bill McGuire, Professor of Geophysical Hazards at University College London, there is a 0.15 per cent probability of it happening during the next 70 years. Likely venues for the eruption include restless calderas that are known to be above still-active hot-spots, and where monitoring shows that the ground is moving – such as the former super-eruption site at Yellowstone. Yellowstone has experienced a super-eruption at roughly regular intervals of 650,000 years, and the last one was … 650,000 years ago. Other candidate calderas include Lake Taupo in New Zealand and the Phlegrean Fields near Naples, Italy. Alternatively any of the world's 3,000 active volcanoes could prove to be sitting on a giant plume of magma sufficient to cause a super-eruption, or such a plume could rise to the surface somewhere else. This is most likely to happen around the Pacific Rim or in South East Asia – leading experts think that the Southern Andes is a possible candidate location.

Would there be any warning?

Ground movements on the flanks of volcanoes can be measured through monitoring stations or by satellite, giving warning of an eruption several days or weeks in advance, but it is necessary to know where to look. Only 150 of the world's 3,000 active volcanoes are monitored, and, furthermore, a super-volcano could erupt in an area that has no history of volcanism. Perhaps in the future scientists will devise a method of detecting the movements of plumes of magma below the Earth's crust, giving plenty of warning of possible eruption venues.

Ultimately, however, monitoring may not be that valuable. While evacuating a threatened region might save lives in the short-term, there is nothing we can do to stop an eruption, and even people on the other side of the globe will suffer the medium–long-term consequences of a volcanic winter and UV spring. The only chance for survival would be through civil defence measures of the sort conceived during the Cold War. Most civil defence infrastructure has been allowed to fall into disrepair since the end of the Cold War, however, and it is hard to see how even the best prepared and stocked bunker could support more than a handful of people for several years. In summary, the relatively high chance of a super-eruption, together with mankind's powerlessness to do anything about it, make a super-volcano one of *the* most serious doomsday threats facing civilisation.

Likelihood: 6

Damage: 10

Fear factor: 7

Mega-tsunami

The Boxing Day tsunami in 2004 showed the terrible destructive power of giant waves crashing onto an unprepared shoreline. But according to a leading expert in geophysical hazards, the heartland of the developed world is in clear and present danger from mega-tsunamis far larger and more destructive than the Boxing Day wave. Professor Bill McGuire warns that a slight ground tremor on a small island off the coast of Africa could unleash monster waves 50 metres high that would wipe out most of the major cities of the North Atlantic rim, from New York and Miami to Lisbon.

Tsunamis are usually produced by submarine earthquakes, which cause part of the seabed to drop or rise suddenly, displacing the ocean above and generating waves that can be 10 metres high or more. This is what happened on Boxing Day, 2004. But much larger waves can be generated when large volumes of rock suddenly fall into the sea, causing huge local displacement. The dome of water thus generated spreads outwards as mega-tsunamis, which can be hundreds of metres high in the immediate vicinity, and, according to some models, are still 10–15 metres high after crossing entire oceans. The waves travel at the speed of a jumbo jet, and if they hit a coastline that is shaped in the right way – eg an estuary or funnel-shaped bay – they can be focused into 50-metre high monsters.

According to Professor McGuire, a mega-tsunami could be triggered by a catastrophic landslide from the sides of an island volcano, such as those in Hawaii or the Canary Islands, off the coast of Northwest Africa. Such volcanoes are often composed of loosely stacked rubble, honeycombed with cracks and tunnels from earthquakes and erosion, which makes them very unstable. An eruption or even a small earthquake could potentially cause the entire side of such a volcano to shear off and slide into the sea in just a few seconds. Cumbre Vieja volcano on La Palma in the Canaries is considered to be the prime candidate. Its western flank, which comprises several hundred cubic kilometres of rock weighing 500 billion tonnes, was slightly displaced during an earthquake in 1949, and McGuire believes that it is poised to slip into the ocean in one mighty landslide.

What will happen if a mega-tsunami is triggered?

According to McGuire and his colleagues at University College, the following scenario could happen tomorrow: magma wells to the surface beneath the fragile, crumbling mass of Cumbre Vieja. Tiny tremors shake the ground, building in intensity until, abruptly, the entire western flank begins to move. Gathering pace it hurtles into the Atlantic Ocean in the space of just a few seconds, displacing a vast dome of water 900 metres high in the centre. As this subsides, massive waves ripple off in all directions. The tsunami is 100 metres high when it hits the other Canary Islands, scouring all signs of life from their densely populated shores. One hour later it hits the coast of Africa, and 5–7 hours later it hits Spain, Ireland and Britain, still 7 metres high.

Travelling westwards the wave retains much of its height. It is tens of metres high when it hits Brazil, six hours after the slide, and 9–12 hours later it smashes into the eastern seaboard of the US, where bays and estuaries funnel it into 50-metre walls of death that devastate Miami, Washington, Baltimore, New York and Boston. Because it has a wavelength hundreds of kilometres long, the wave does not simply hit the shoreline and recede – it keeps on coming, for as long as 15 minutes or more, travelling far inland, before retreating (which means a vast flood travelling in the other direction for 15 minutes+).

Assuming that the initial landslide on La Palma was noticed, North America would have, at most, 12 hours warning – other targets even less. Only a fraction of the tens of millions of residents of the coastal planes and cities could be evacuated in time. The rest would almost certainly die. The complete destruction of many of the major cities in the developed world would destroy the world economy at a stroke. Civilisation might not collapse but it would be changed forever.

Has it happened before?

Island volcano collapses triggered mega-tsunamis at Unzen in Japan in 1792, and at Ritter Island in New Britain (near Papua New Guinea) in 1808. On both occasions, thousands died. There is evidence of even bigger collapses and mega-tsunamis in prehistoric times. Scans of the seabed around the Hawaiian Islands reveal the debris of 70 huge landslides, some involving over 1,000 cubic kilometres of rock. These have been linked to deposition of marine material 300 metres above sea level on neighbouring islands, and to evidence for the impact of a 15-metre tsunami on New South Wales in Australia on the other side of the ocean. Similarly there is evidence of prehistoric landslides on the Canary Islands, such as huge friction scars on the island of El Hierro, and of mega-tsunamis that crossed the ocean, in the form of giant boulders lifted 20 metres above sea level in the Bahamas. A landslide on volcanic Réunion Island, in the Indian Ocean, is thought to have triggered a mega-tsunami that reshaped the coastline of the nearby island of Madagascar 4,000 years ago.

Civilisation and tsunamis

Tsunamis caused by volcanic eruptions may have ended civilisations in the past. The legend of Atlantis tells of an island empire that was entirely swallowed by huge waves during a cataclysm of earthquakes and volcanoes, and may represent some sort of folk memory of real events, such as the impact of the explosion of Thera (now called Santorini) on the Minoan civilisation. Whether or not this enormous eruption, (thought to be as big as the Tambora VEI7 eruption of 1815) genuinely caused the collapse of the Minoans is hotly contested. Proxy records (such as tree rings and ice cores) seem to date the eruption to around 1630 BCE, while archaeological remains seem to date the fall of the Minoans to 1450 BCE, but many argue that one or other of these dates is wrong. There is evidence that the enormous tsunami produced by Thera destroyed the Minoan fleet, and it must have done terrible damage to coastal communities.

How likely is it to happen?

According to McGuire and his colleagues, Cumbre Vieja is poised to collapse at any moment, while similar landslides could occur on the Hawaiian Islands or Réunion Island, triggering mega-tsunamis in the Pacific or Indian oceans. McGuire estimates that, on average, a mega-tsunami is unleashed once every 10,000 years. Climate change is likely to produce more and heavier bursts of rain on tropical volcanic islands such as the Canaries, Hawaii and Réunion, which means more erosion, more instability of volcano flanks and a greater probability of catastrophic collapse.

Mega-tsunami sceptics

Not everyone agrees with McGuire's theories, however. Recent research by the Southampton Oceanography Centre suggests that volcanic island collapses tend to be gradual rather than catastrophic. They claim that sediment cores from the sea floor around Cumbre Vieja show that past landslides have been small and frequent, and therefore that there is little risk of a catastrophic collapse of the entire western flank of the volcano. Instead, it is likely to fall into the ocean in a series of small landslides, rather than the enormous collapse posited by McGuire. Even if they are wrong and he is right, the eastern seaboard of the US may not be in danger. According to the Hawaii-based Tsunami Society, landslide-triggered mega-tsunamis are purely local phenomena, and unlike earthquake-triggered tsunami would not propagate across vast distances.

Keeping watch

McGuire insists that the threat to America and elsewhere is real and needs to be taken seriously. He argues that the US government, and others, need to put in place plans for an enormous evacuation operation. Such an operation would take weeks, and thus would only work if there were adequate warning of an imminent island collapse. As McGuire told the BBC: 'We need to be out there now looking at when an eruption is likely to happen ... otherwise there will be no time to evacuate major cities.'

At present there is no adequate monitoring of Cumbre Vieja. Seismometers would only pick up a quake or eruption once it had happened, and by then it might be too late – the wave could already be on its way, leaving America less than twelve hours to prepare for impact. A proper monitoring system that could warn of major activity weeks in advance would not cost much, but given the uncertainty over the science behind the mega-tsunami threat, and the sceptical voices, is it likely that hard-pressed governments will pay for one? It is surely even less likely that they would be willing to trigger the largest mass evacuation (and mass panic) in history on the basis of a contested theory.

The competing claims make it hard to evaluate the true risk of a doomsday mega-tsunami. On balance it seems that there is enough uncertainty to put this scenario low down on the list of concerns. We won't really know until there is an eruption on Cumbre Vieja, or an unexpected collapse on another island volcano, and McGuire's vindication would come at a terrible price.

Likelihood: 2
Damage: 4
Fear factor: 3

Reversal of the Poles

In the recent film *The Core*, scientists must race against time to avert a reversal of the Earth's magnetic poles before the planet is exposed to the full glare of solar radiation. Although the science of the film was widely derided by experts, it did highlight a genuine concern. There is strong evidence that the Earth's magnetic field (aka the geomagnetic field) is weakening, prior to a flip, and nobody knows for certain how dangerous this could prove.

Life on Earth is possible because our planet has a strong magnetic field, which is generated by currents in the molten core. The field stretches out into space, where it acts as a magnetic shield (known as the magnetosphere), protecting the Earth's surface from the constant bombardment of highly energetic particles streaming out from the Sun (the solar wind). The magnetosphere deflects most of these particles into space, although sometimes streams of them follow the lines of magnetic force down to the Earth's magnetic poles. When they hit the atmosphere, they generate the light shows known as the auroras.

Like an ordinary magnet, the Earth's magnetic field has two poles, which roughly coincide with the geographical North and South Poles. The magnetic orientation of rock formed at different times in Earth's history shows, however, that the current orientation is far from permanent. The magnetic poles have reversed many times in history, at irregularly spaced intervals. Sometimes an orientation persists for millions of years; at others, it lasts for only a few thousand. A reversal usually takes a few thousand years, preceded by a period when the geomagnetic field weakens and fails. There is mounting evidence that this is exactly what is happening at the moment.

What will happen if the Earth's magnetic field fails?

It is important to note that it is the potential weakening/failure of the geomagnetic field that is the real concern, rather than the pole reversal that might follow, because with a weakened or non-existent geomagnetic field, the magnetosphere would weaken or disappear. The solar wind would no longer be deflected from the planet, and would instead hit the upper atmosphere. Most of the particles would get no further, but there could be a significant increase in the number of highly energetic particles that penetrate to the Earth's surface, especially during sun storms.

Solar particles could do a lot of damage. They could damage the ozone layer, which might thin dramatically during a sun storm. The thinning could take years to heal up, allowing dangerous UV radiation to bathe the planet, harming crops and animals and causing cancer and conjunctivitis in humans. Solar particles themselves can damage DNA and increase the risk of cancer; they can also short-circuit electrical equipment.

Even a slight weakening of the Earth's magnetic field exposes orbiting satellites to particle bombardment, causing malfunctions and meltdown. Solar storms can sometimes penetrate a full strength magnetosphere to cause severe problems on Earth, such as power outages and blackouts. If the geomagnetic field failed altogether, all satellites and possibly all telecommunications and electricity-transfer technology would be inoperable. Civilisation might falter without them.

The natural world could also suffer, as many creatures – from bacteria and bumblebees to turtles and whales – rely on the orientation of the geomagnetic field for navigation. With a weakened field they would be unable to find their way to breeding grounds, or even to negotiate their local environment; many species would be decimated and the delicate balance of the global ecosystem might be upset.

All this is entirely speculative, however. The truth is that no one really knows what a geomagnetic shutdown might portend. Humans have never been around to observe one, and the legacy of past failures is debated. Most scientists think that the natural world would be able to cope. Eventually (after 5,000–7,000 years) the Earth's magnetic field would return, possibly in the opposite orientation to today, and life could get back to normal with some slight adaptations. Whether our hi-tech civilisation would survive the period of geomagnetic inactivity is less certain.

Has it happened before?

Weakening of the geomagnetic field has occurred repeatedly throughout the Earth's history – sometimes leading to a full reversal of the poles, and sometimes simply returning to full strength along its previous orientation (known as a geomagnetic excursion). On average, pole reversals happen every 250,000 years, and it has been 780,000 years since the last one, but such a large interval is not unusual. During the Cretaceous era, when the dinosaurs ruled the Earth, there were no pole reversals for 30 million years. There may well have been significant fluctuations or even excursions since the last reversal.

Did past reversals and excursions affect life on Earth? Research in the 1970s suggested that extinctions of species of tiny marine organisms called radiolarians coincided with past pole reversals, but this has since been put down to faulty statistics. Most palaeontologists don't think reversals and excursions have caused extinctions, and obviously our ancestors survived the last reversal adequately. On the other hand, there were no satellites, power grids or other electrical technology back then.

How likely is it to happen?

Satellite measurements show that the Earth's magnetic field *is* getting weaker. So far it has deteriorated by 10–15 per cent, and if it continues to decline at this rate it will disappear by 4000 CE, possibly even as early as 3000 CE, because there is some evidence that the decline is accelerating. Local fluctuations in the geomagnetic field are common, but the overall decline means that some regions of the Earth – such as near the North Pole and just below South Africa – now have a particularly weak field. This weakness extends out to the magnetosphere. Over South Africa the strength of the magnetosphere has declined by 30 per cent, exposing satellites that pass through this region of space to a barrage of solar radiation.

None of this evidence is conclusive, however. Fluctuations in the overall geomagnetic field are routine, and so far the decline is within the normal range of variation. Even if the field decays a lot further, it may not disappear altogether, and even if it does, few scientists subscribe to the extreme dooms-day scenario outlined above. The consensus seems to be that the magnetosphere would persist and that only during solar storms would solar particles threaten the ozone layer and the Earth's surface. On balance, a geomagnetic excursion or rever-sal is more likely to be a nuisance than a catastrophe.

Likelihood: 6
Damage: 1
Fear factor: 1

Cosmological catastrophes

The Universe is generally a hostile place for living things, bathed in radiation and energetic particles that can destroy the fragile chemicals that make up organisms and the envi-ronment in which they can flourish. Even our own Sun pumps out streams of dangerous UV radiation and energetic particles. Only because of our planet's magnetosphere and ozone layer is life on the surface protected from these killers. But even these planetary shields would not be enough to pro-tect us from the huge blasts of deadly radiation which can be released by cosmological cataclysms.

The main cosmological threats are gamma-ray bursts and blasts of cosmic rays. Gamma rays are a form of highly energetic electromagnetic radiation (akin to visible light, UV and X-rays). Cosmic rays are very energetic particles that can pass through entire planets, but which occasionally smash into another atom with as much energy as a particle accelerator impact (see Chapter 1), creating highly reactive ions. Both gamma and cosmic rays could come from a number of sources – some of which have only recently been discovered by astronomical science – including star-quakes, star collapses leading to black hole formation, neutron star collisions and supernovae.

Star-quakes

Star-quakes are a hypothetical phenomenon thought to occur on magnetars – super-magnetic neutron stars (stars composed entirely of neutrons). Magnetars are so densely packed that they assume an almost crystalline structure. They are under enormous stress from the vast gravitational force they produce and the immense speed at which they rotate. Occasionally the crystalline structure undergoes a sudden, catastrophic reorganisation, analogous to an earthquake. The star-quake sets off a hugely powerful flare, which in turn releases a burst of gamma rays. More energy is released in a tenth of a second than our Sun produces in 100,000 years. Storms of cosmic rays would then follow after the gamma-ray bursts.

Star collapses and star collisions

Even more powerful gamma-ray bursts have been observed, during which as much energy is released in just a few seconds as our Sun emits in its entire lifetime. These bursts are believed to result from stars collapsing in on themselves to form black holes, or from collisions between neutron stars. Again, gamma-ray bursts would be followed by storms of cosmic rays that can last for months.

Supernovas

Huge showers of cosmic rays are also released when a large star reaches the end of its life and blows itself apart in a final, enormous explosion, creating a supernova. The expanding shell of gas left over from the supernova can continue to emit cosmic rays for thousands of years.

What will happen if there is a cosmological catastrophe near us?

A big enough burst of radiation could blast away the Earth's atmosphere, boil the oceans and fry everything on the face of the planet. It is more likely, however, that a gamma-ray burst or shower of cosmic rays would be mainly soaked up by the upper atmosphere. This could have nonetheless devastating impact on life. Gamma and cosmic rays would ionise nitrogen and oxygen in the atmosphere, which would then combine to give nitrogen dioxide – more familiar to us as one of the components of smog, and a potent destroyer of ozone. A gamma-ray burst, or the extended shower of cosmic rays that would follow such a burst or arrive from a supernova, would generate a thick screen of smog all around the planet, devastating the ozone layer. As with an asteroid impact or super-volcano, global dimming would lead to a cosmic winter, and would be followed in turn by a UV spring.

According to Dr Adrian Melott, of the University of Kansas, just a 10-second burst of gamma rays would destroy half of the ozone layer, and five years later there would still be 10 per cent missing. According to Narcisco Benítez of John Hopkins University in Baltimore, Maryland, cosmic rays from a super-nova near Earth could create a global smog that would last up to 1,000 years. Some scientists believe that such events trigger major periods of cooling, leading to Ice Ages. Dramatic cooling and high levels of radiation would make the Earth's surface inhospitable. Civilisation would crumble and the survival of the human species would be in doubt.

Has it happened before?

Some palaeontologists suspect that gamma-ray bursts may have been responsible for major extinction events. In partic-ular, gamma rays are prime suspects in the Ordovician extinction, some 450 million years ago, when 60 per cent of marine invertebrates were wiped out (at a time when there were few other creatures in existence). More recently, there is evidence that a nearby supernova could have been linked to a big die-off of marine molluscs that occurred 2 million years ago. At this time the Earth passed relatively close to a cluster of supernovae, and ocean-floor deposits of a rare isotope of iron – of the sort blown off supernovae – date to the same period. Gamma- and cosmic-ray bursts are also thought to have been responsible for triggering some of the periods in Earth's history when the planet was cooler and Ice Ages were frequent.

How likely is it to happen?

Gamma-ray bursts happen several times a day, and supernovae are found all over the Universe, but fortunately one would have to go off quite close to our Solar System (in astronomical terms) for us to be affected. For the Earth to be threatened we would have to be within 6,000 light years of a gamma-ray burst, 130 light years of a supernova or 10 light years of a star-quake. As far as astronomers know, there are no magnetars anywhere near us in the galaxy, and the nearest star known to be at risk of going supernova is 500 light years away. According to Nir Shaviv, a senior lecturer in physics at the Hebrew University in Jerusalem, Israel, 'The Earth is at greatest risk when it passes through a spiral arm of the Milky Way, where most of the supernovae occur' – and this is not due to happen for another 60 million years.

John Scalo and Craig Wheeler of the University of Texas at Austin estimate that gamma-ray bursts occur close enough to Earth to affect it once every 5 million years, but since the origins of the bursts remain mysterious the current danger to the Earth is unclear. In November 2004 NASA launched the Swift space telescope to search for and observe gamma-ray bursts. Swift may provide more information on the true sources of such bursts and whether there are any close to the Earth. Since there is nothing that mankind could do to avert a gamma-ray burst doomsday, however, there is little point in worrying about the remote probability of one happening anytime soon.

Likelihood: 0.5
Damage: 10
Fear factor: 1

Runaway stars and wandering black holes

Celestial objects don't have to explode to threaten the Earth. Astronomers have detected several types of 'wandering' object, including black holes, stars and brown dwarfs (giant balls of gas similar to very large Jupiter-like planets, but not quite big enough to become stars). Instead of being locked into a stable orbit in a solar system or around the centre of a galaxy, these objects follow eccentric orbits or simply speed through space. It is conceivable that one of them could blunder into our Solar System.

What will happen if the Earth encounters a wandering celestial object?

Contrary to popular myth, a black hole would not suck the Earth into its ravenous maw – at least not unless it passed extremely close to us. However, the mere presence of a large and gravitationally significant foreign body, such as a black hole, star or brown dwarf, would completely disrupt the current order of the Solar System. The asteroid belt and the Oort Cloud would be disturbed, sending debris hurtling through the system in all directions, and the planets themselves would be dragged out of their orbits. This could cause disastrous tidal upheavals both on the surface of the Earth and beneath it, leading to massive flooding, earthquakes and eruptions. More importantly, the distance between the Earth and the Sun would be changed, so that the planet would either be cooked or would freeze.

Has it happened before?

The current order of the Solar System shows that it has never been disturbed by errant celestial visitors.

How likely is it to happen?

Astronomers rate the chances of a black hole, star or brown dwarf wandering into the Solar System as extremely low. It is almost certain that the Sun will run out of fuel and turn into a red giant, destroying the Earth in the process, before such an astronomically unlikely event occurs.

Likelihood: 0.0000001
Damage: 10
Fear factor: 0.000001

Conclusion: The end of the world is nigh?

Only one of the doomsday scenarios in this chapter definitely threatens civilisation: a super-volcanic eruption. The other scenarios are either too unlikely or too contentious: the chances of being hit by an asteroid or comet too big to be deflected or destroyed are slim; the threat of island collapses and the reach of mega-tsunamis are disputed; a pole-reversal probably wouldn't be disastrous; and the probability of a cosmological catastrophe or wandering celestial object manifesting near enough to the Earth is almost certainly astronomically remote.

Sooner or later, however, a super-volcano will come along, and what makes it so terrifying is that, unlike the man-made problems afflicting our ecosystem, there will be nothing we can do about it, and no way we can ameliorate its cataclysmic effects. So, perhaps the message of this chapter is gloomy – the end of Earth civilisation as we know it *is* inevitable. On the other hand, that end is not necessarily nigh. The odds are good that none of the cataclysms covered in this chapter will endanger you or your descendants for many generations to come. Alarming though they may be, they should be seen in the context of the far more realistic threat from ecocide and global warming. Not only are these doomsday scenarios disturbingly likely, they are also *worth* worrying about because we *can* do something about them.

Conclusion

Of the 29 doomsday scenarios detailed in this book, only a handful are genuinely likely to threaten civilisation, but these few are worrying enough. Top of the list is undoubtedly the looming ecological disaster that our unsustainable consumption looks set to unleash. Whether through triggering global warming or simply stripping the planet's assets, the prevailing consumerist-capitalist model of our civilisation seems to be setting us on course for disaster. The classical illustration of this argument is the 'tragedy of the commons'.

The tragedy of the commons

The tragedy of the commons refers to a scenario where a group of farmers all have the right to graze their cattle on a common. If each farmer limits the grazing done by his cow, there will be plenty of grass to go round and the common will sustain all the cows. If one farmer lets his cow graze more than the limit, no great harm will be done – his cow will get fatter than the others but they will still have enough to eat. So it pays for individual farmers to ignore the limits. In fact, if a farmer does not ignore the limits he will be at a disadvantage – the common will still be grazed out, but his cow will be thin and wasted while the others grow fat off his share. So in fact it pays for all the farmers to overgraze their cows, even though this is unsustainable in the long-term and eventually all the farmers will lose out. The same argument can be applied to common resources such as fisheries or forestry, and this is exactly what we see in the world around us. For instance, many European fisheries are currently over-exploited, but it makes no sense for, say, Scottish fishermen to stay in port and not fish if fleets of Portuguese trawlers are simply going to snap up all of their catch anyway.

In his book *Collapse*, Jared Diamond describes a historical example of how the tragedy of the commons can bring down a society. Easter Island originally possessed an abundance of trees that formed the basis of a rich ecosystem, capable of sustaining a substantial human population in a complex society of competing tribes ruled by kings. This society developed a model of kingship where a king's authority derived from the size of the statues they were able to erect, a process that consumed unsustainable quantities of timber. If a king had tried to conserve timber resources by not erecting statues, he would have been deposed or defeated by one who would. The system was inherently unsustainable. By the 16th century CE the island was deforested, and soon after the ecosystem collapsed and with it, society. When European explorers arrived they discovered a sparse population eking out a miserable existence on a desolate, barren wasteland.

Admittedly my retelling of this story is heavily simplified, but the parallels between Easter Island and our situation today are irresistible. The corporations that mediate the consumerist-capitalist model are like the Easter Island kings of old: any corporation that tries to sacrifice its bottom line in order to avoid short-termism and conserve resources will not only be at a competitive disadvantage with other companies, but will actually be in breach of is legal responsibilities to its share-holders. The parallel is even closer for our political leaders: any prime minister or president who voluntarily sacrifices his or her country's prosperity for the greater good of the planet will soon be replaced by the voters with one who maintains economic growth and prosperity.

Averting disaster

A lot of people are sceptical of this consumerism-capitalism bashing, and there are many arguments that explain why this model won't lead to disaster. For instance, Diamond points out that not all societies succumb to the tragedy of the commons. Some achieve a degree of collective responsibility, whereby all the stakeholders abide by self-imposed regulation. Others, including in theory our own, depend on control from above, in the form of government, which can take a disinterested, long-term view. To put these options another way, you could argue that disaster will be averted through a combination of free market economics on the one hand, and enlightened regulation by governments and international bodies on the other.

Neither of these 'rescue' options inspires much confidence. For the forces of the market to regulate themselves it will be necessary for the global economy to adopt a 'true cost' approach, where resources, processes, etc, are properly costed in terms of their value to or impact on the environment. Petrol, for instance, would increase massively in price to reflect the cost of carbon emissions. The price of meat, to give another example, would have to reflect the true cost of producing it, including the grain and water required and the effluent produced, the wild habitat cleared for ranching, the emissions produced in shipping it, the health consequences incurred by the added hormones, etc, etc.

At the moment most of the costs are simply externalised by damaging the environment without paying for it. There are a few signs that things are beginning to change, such as the European Union Emissions Trading Scheme (see page 165) or rising fuel duties in some countries, but adopting an effective 'true cost' regime would arguably cripple the world economy. High petrol prices, for instance, can be a major cause of recession. Neither voters nor consumers will pay higher prices and sacrifice living standards willingly, and, as already discussed, corporations cannot voluntarily undermine their bottom line – they must, by their nature, externalise costs as much as possible.

What of the 'top down' approach? Will international treaties or supra-governmental bodies save us? The evidence of recent years suggests not. The world's major current and future polluters did not sign up to Kyoto, and at the time of writing it looks unlikely that even the very limited aims of the 2005 G8 summit will be realised. This is not simply an issue of American intransigence or the 'big bad Bush'. Most commentators agree that the effects of globalisation have been to strengthen the hand of multi-national corporations and weaken the power of governments – moving us further away from the possibility of the sort of world government with genuine authority that is the only solution to a global-scale tragedy of the commons.

The march of science

A common fallback argument of consumerist-capitalist supporters is that technological advances will make current rates of consumption ecologically viable, particularly as the economic imperatives for innovation strengthen. But this argument is also suspect. Technology rarely solves more problems than it causes, and new technologies take decades to come on stream anyway, especially if they are to be adopted on a global scale (eg replacing petrol with hydrogen). The threat to civilisation is from forces at work now, which will take their worst toll in the next few decades. Technological succour would almost certainly come too late.

Believing that technology will save us is more an article of faith than a realistic hope, based in part on an assumption that a society as complex and advanced as our own will be immune to the disasters that befell past civilisations. This assumption is ill-founded. The history of collapsed societies shows that it was often at the point of peak size, power, complexity and attainment that they reached the tipping point beyond which their environment could no longer support them, and that subsequent collapse was almost immediate, rather than a gradual decline.

What can you do?

As an individual your ability to change the course of global society is limited, but on the other hand, every little helps. There is not really the space here for a detailed discussion of sustainable living, but based on the scenarios outlined in this book, here is a quick guide to reducing your ecological footprint and saving the planet:

- *Live green*: Save energy and water; recycle.

- *Travel green*: Cycle and use public transport, avoid unnecessary car journeys and car pool/share where possible; don't fly anywhere.

- *Eat green*: Avoid meat, eat only MSC fish, eat organic (look for Soil Association certification).

- *Go local*: Buy local products and services wherever possible; don't go abroad for holidays.

- *Consume ethically*: Buy ethical products and services (eg fair trade foods, FSC wood).

- *Use the ballot box*: Vote for parties with green agendas and people who are committed to binding international treaties; lobby for these where possible; get involved with grass roots organisations.

- *Think green*: Educate yourself and others; support research and activism.

Easter Island Earth

Even if you adhere to all these guidelines, your influence will be limited, and no amount of ethical living will help to avert potential geophysical catastrophes such as asteroid impact or super-volcanic eruption. The balanced view must be that a negative outcome is very, very likely. Throughout the book I've surveyed the possible consequences of the various doomsday scenarios. Based on all the evidence, is it possible to select the most likely elements from these scenarios and give a picture of what the world might be like 50 years from now?

'He who lives by the crystal ball soon learns to eat ground glass,' warned Edgar R Fielder, but here are some broad predictions nonetheless. In the developed world, standards of living and quality of life will fall dramatically, while the developing world will collapse into chronic famine, war and disease, far worse than today's problems. Life expectancy will fall for everyone, partly because levels of risk will increase radically. Even the developed world will be at chronically higher risk from wild weather, disease, war and terrorism. The gulf between the rich and the poor will increase, both globally and within countries, including developed ones. There will be greater injustice and an erosion of cultural values, with more authoritarian and even totalitarian regimes. There will also be considerable bitterness about the profligacy of earlier generations.

In a worst-case scenario, Earth could come to resemble Easter Island on a planetary scale. Aliens arriving a few centuries from now will marvel at the monumental remains of a mighty civilisation, and ponder how they could have been created by the scattered pockets of humans eking out a miserable existence in a barren, toxic wasteland practically empty of resources. Their archaeologists will be shocked to discover that this cyclopean culture ruled a world of incredible natural riches that disappeared just a few hundreds years ago. The chilling tale will be purveyed to alien students as an object lesson in the perils of unsustainable living.

Prepare for the worst

If you take these warnings seriously, what should you do? What might be the best place to live, for instance, to minimise the odds of being caught up in doomsday and to maximise your chances of survival? Obviously a lot depends on the exact nature of the doomsday scenario. The first tip would be to move away from low-lying areas, particularly the coast. Rising sea levels are almost inevitable given the likely course of global warming, while tsunamis can be expected to follow asteroid impact, island collapse, methane sediment release or super-volcanic eruption near or in the ocean. The second tip would be to move to high latitudes. Warming is quite likely to make the Tropics unbearably hot, but high latitude regions such as the Canadian or Siberian tundra may actually become more hospitable. Having said which, a third tip might be to avoid the Northern Hemisphere altogether. Warming (and cooling, in a new Ice Age scenario) is expected to hit the Northern Hemisphere particularly hard, while most pollution is produced there too. There are also more people, which could make it more dangerous in the event of conflict and instability – a nuclear war, for instance, is likely to affect the Northern Hemisphere primarily. New Zealand might be a good option – its climate should remain hospitable in the face of global warming, and many parts of it are well equipped with water, good soil and other resources. There aren't too many people already there, and it is isolated enough to make it difficult for armies of desperate refugees to reach.

But geographical tips are only useful to a limited extent. Most of the doomsday scenarios envisage negative impacts spreading all over the globe eventually. Atmospheric and ocean circulation mean that heat, pollution, dust, debris, fall-out, etc will eventually be carried all round the planet. History shows that the people best equipped to survive a catastrophe are those who are flexible and resourceful, and who can call on a network of support from family and neighbours. On this basis, you might be better off in a region with good links to other parts of the world, where survivors are more likely to receive aid and assistance from others, than somewhere isolated such as New Zealand. You will also boost your chances of survival if you learn the skills needed for a self-reliant, low-tech future, such as farming and basic crafts.

Conclusion

The last word

Most authors writing on the topic of doomsday seek to end on a positive note, offering at least a glimmer of hope that, through a combination of luck, grass roots activism and visionary statesmanship, the worst may be avoided and society will find a way out of the mire. I wish I could be so optimistic. Neither history nor current trends suggest that solutions will be found to global problems until it is too late. I look to the future with a wary eye.

References

Internet articles

In the fast-moving world of doomsday research, new stories and studies come out on a daily basis, making the Internet an invaluable resource. Two of the best sites for accessible, up-to-date information about the whole range of doomsday scenarios are the *New Scientist* website (www.newscientist.com), and the BBC's Planet in Peril sites (http://news.bbc.co.uk/1/hi/in_depth/sci_tech/2004/planet/default.stm).

Here is a selection of important internet articles referenced in the text:

'African droughts "triggered by Western pollution"'; Rachel Nowak; NewScientist.com; 12/6/02; www.newscientist.com/article.ns?id=dn2393

'Aid agencies' warning on climate'; Alex Kirby; BBC News Online; 20/10/04; http://news.bbc.co.uk/go/pr/fr/-/1/hi/sci/tech/3756642.stm

'Can the world go on as it is?'; Megan Lane; BBC News Online; 18/8/03; http://news.bbc.co.uk/go/pr/fr/-/1/hi/magazine/3153661.stm

'Causes for concern: Chemicals and wildlife'; Valerie Brown; WWF; December 2003; http://www.worldwildlife.org/toxics/pubs/causesforconcern.pdf

'Climate change sceptics "wrong"'; Richard Black; BBC News Online; 18/11/04; http://news.bbc.co.uk/go/pr/fr/-/1/hi/uk/4021197.stm

'Climate warning from the deep'; Julianna Kettlewell; BBC News Online; 12/7/04; http://news.bbc.co.uk/go/pr/fr/-/1/hi/sci/tech/3879841.stm

'Dissecting flu's deadly weaponry'; Rachael Buchanan; BBC News Online; 13/12/04; http://news.bbc.co.uk/go/pr/fr/-/1/hi/sci/tech/4092709.stm

'Double whammy link to extinctions'; Paul Rincon; BBC News Online; 1/4/05; http://news.bbc.co.uk/go/pr/fr/-/1/hi/sci/tech/3582767.stm

'Expert slams wave threat inertia'; BBC News Online; 10/8/04; http://news.bbc.co.uk/go/pr/fr/-/1/hi/sci/tech/3553368.stm

'Exporting Harm: The Hi-Tech trashing of Asia'; Silicon Valley Toxics Coalition; Feb 2002; www.svtc.org/cleancc/pubs/technotrash.pdf

'Flood basalts, mantle plumes and mass extinctions'; Steve Self and Mike Rampino; *The Geological Society*; no date; www.geolsoc.org.uk/template.cfm?name=fbasalts

'Greenhouse gases "do warm oceans"'; Paul Rincon; BBC News Online; 17/2/05; http://news.bbc.co.uk/go/pr/fr/-/1/hi/sci/tech/4275729.stm

'Huge "star-quake" rocks Milky Way'; BBC News Online; 18/2/05; http://news.bbc.co.uk/go/pr/fr/-/1/hi/sci/tech/4278005.stm

'Industry "denies chemical risks"'; BBC News Online; 2/12/04; http://news.bbc.co.uk/go/pr/fr/-/1/hi/sci/tech/4058389.stm

'Is money fighting climate change well spent?'; Andrew Walker; BBC News Online; 14/12/04; http://news.bbc.co.uk/

References

go/pr/fr/-/1/hi/business/4094589.stm

'It's seven minutes to midnight'; *Bulletin of the Atomic Scientists* website; March/April 2002; www.thebulletin.org/doomsday_clock/current_time.htm

'Lab fireball "may be black hole"'; BBC News Online; 17/3/05; http://news.bbc.co.uk/go/pr/fr/-/1/hi/sci/tech/4357613.stm

'Mega-tsunami hazards'; *The Tsunami Society*; 15/1/03; www.sthjournal.org/media.htm

'Natural Catastrophes During Bronze Age Civilisations: Archaeological, geological, astronomical and cultural perspectives: Introduction'; Benny J Peiser, Trevor Palmer and Mark E Bailey; *Proceedings of the Second SIS Cambridge Conference*; July 1997; www.knowledge.co.uk/sis/cambproc.htm#intro

'Only huge emissions cuts will curb climate change'; Jenny Hogan; Newscientist.com news service; 3/2/05; www.newscientist.com/article.ns?id=dn6964

'Ozone loss caused genetic mutations at time of mass extinction'; *The Ozone Hole* website; 26/7/04; www.theozone-hole.com/ozoneloss.htm

'Paving the planet'; Lester R Brown; *San Diego Earth Times*; March 2001; www.sdearthtimes.com/et0301/et0301s7.html

'Pest resistance to pesticides'; Robert Bellinger, Clemson University; March 1996; http://entweb.clemson.edu/pesticid/Issues/pestrest.pdf

'Planet in peril: Humans push natural systems to the brink'; Duncan Graham-Rowe and Bob Holmes; New Scientist.com news service; 2/4/05; www.newscientist.com/channel/earth/mg18624934.300

'Pollution: A life and death issue'; BBC News online, 13/12/04; http://news.bbc.co.uk/go/pr/fr/-/1/hi/sci/tech/4086809.stm

'Report: Child asthma rates double'; Associated Press; CNN.com; 24 February, 2003; http://www.cnn.com/2003/HEALTH/02/24/children.pollution.ap

'Scientists Warn of Risk from Doomsday Asteroids'; Deborah Zabarenko; 27/7/99; www.space.com/scienceastronomy/astronomy/doomsday.html

'Sewage waters a tenth of world's irrigated crops'; Fred Pierce; NewScientist.com, 18/8/04; www.newscientist.com/article.ns?id=dn6297

'Taking soybeans to new depths'; Indiana Soybean Board; 14/4/05; http://www.indianasoybeanboard.com/Aquaculture.shtml

'The influenza pandemic of 1918'; Molly Billings; June 1997; www.stanford.edu/group/virus/uda/

'The effects of nuclear weapons'; CND website; April 2001; www.cnduk.org/pages/binfo/effects.html

The Starving Ocean; Debbie MacKenzie; www.fisherycrisis.com

'Tidal wave threat "over-hyped"'; Ali Ayres; BBC News Online; 29/10/04; http://news.bbc.co.uk/go/pr/fr/-/1/hi/sci/tech/3963563.stm

'Traffic fumes "kill 20,000 people a year in Europe"'; Paul Brown; Guardian Unlimited; 1/9/00; www.guardian.co.uk/Archive/Article/0,4273,4057715,00.html

'What a way to go'; Kate Ravilious; Guardian Unlimited; 14/4/05; www.guardian.co.uk/life/feature/story/0,,1458536,00.html

'Whatever happened to machines that think?'; Justin Mullins; New Scientist website; 23/4/05; www.newscientist.com/channel/info-tech/mg18624961.700

References

Print articles

Here is a selection of print articles referenced in the text:

'"Too little" oil for global warming'; Andy Coghlan; *New Scientist*; 5/10/03

'Climate change: Menace or myth?'; Fred Pearce; *New Scientist*; 12/2/05

'Could an even bigger disaster strike in our lifetime?'; Stuart Wavell; *The Sunday Times*; 2/1/05

'Critical thinking about energy'; Thomas R Casten and Brennan Downes; *Skeptical Inquirer* magazine: Volume 29, Number 1, January/February 2005

'Doomsday fears at RHIC'; Thomas Gutierrez; *Skeptical Inquirer*; May 2000

'Flirting with Armageddon: Welcome to a news arms race'; Paul Harris and Jason Burke; *Observer*; 20/2/05

'Gamma rays may have devastated life on Earth'; *New Scientist*; 24/9/03

'Home fires in India help to melt Arctic icecap half a world away'; Geoffrey Lean; *Independent on Sunday*; 3/4/05

'Lights, camera, Armageddon'; Josh Schollmeyer; *Bulletin of the Atomic Scientists*; May/June 2005; pp. 42–50 (vol. 61, no. 03)

'New strains of superbug can kill in 24 hours'; Clara Penn; *Observer*; 20/2/05

'Sleeping giants'; *New Scientist*; 12/2/05

'Superbug has ancestor from 1950s outbreak'; Nigel Hawkes; *The Times*; 1/4/05

'Supernova "smoking gun" linked to mass extinctions'; Eugenie Samuel; *New Scientist*; 9/1/02

'The day after tomorrow'; Richard Girling; *The Sunday Times*

Magazine; 27/3/05

'The temple at the end of time'; John Rowe; *Strange Attractor Journal Two*; 2005

'Tombstone vigilantes ride shotgun to keep the strangers out'; Chris Ayres; *The Times*; 1/4/05

'Uncovering the keys to the lost Indus Cities'; Jonathan Mark Kenoyer; *Scientific American* Volume 15, Number 1, Special Edition; 2005

'Will Compasses Point South?'; William J Broad; *New York Times*; 13/7/04

Books

Diamond, Jared *Collapse: How societies choose to fail or survive*; Penguin Allen Lane: London; 2005

Diamond, Jared *Guns, Germs and Steel*; Vintage: London; 1998

Fagan, Brian *The Little Ice Age*; Basic Books: NY; 2000

Fagan, Brian *The Long Summer*; Granta Books: London; 2004

Levy, Joel *Secret History: Hidden Forces that Shaped the Past*; Vision: London; 2004

McGuire, Bill *A Guide to the End of the World*; OUP: Oxford; 2002

Index

Index

Index

Index

Index

About the Author

Joel Levy is a writer on science, psychology, history and the paranormal, and the author of several books, including: *Secret History* – hidden forces that shaped the past; *Really Useful* – the history and science of everyday things; *Boost Your Brain Power* – a guide to testing and improving your mental abilities, from memory and problem-solving to creativity and emotional intelligence; *Scam: Secrets of the Con Artist* – an inside look at the world and history of the con artist and his scams; *KISS Guide to the Unexplained* – a beginner's guide to historical secrets and mysteries, the paranormal and supernatural; and *Fabulous Creatures* – on creatures of myth and folklore.